Receiving Divine Revelation

Fuchsia Pickett

CREATION HOUSE
Orlando, FL

Creation House
Strang Communications Company
600 Rinehart Road
Lake Mary, FL 32746
Phone: 407-333-3132
Fax: 407-333-7100
Web site: http://www.creationhouse.com

Unless otherwise noted, all Scripture quotations are
from the King James Version of the Bible.

Scripture quotations marked AMP are from
the Amplified Bible. Old Testament
copyright © 1954, 1958, 1987 by the Lockman
Foundation. Used by permission.

Scripture quotations marked NAS are from the New
American Standard Bible. Copyright © 1960, 1962,
1963, 1968, 1971, 1972, 1973, 1975, 1977 by the
Lockman Foundation. Used by permission.

This book is dedicated to
my grandchildren:
Darrell W. Parrish II
Daniel George Parrish
Cyndi Parrish Miller

And in memory of my grandson:
David Parrish

And to my great-grandchildren:
Darrell W. Parrish III
Alysia Parrish
Susan Sermons
Jamie Sermons

CONTENTS

I cease not to give thanks for you, making mention of you in my prayers; that the God of our Lord Jesus Christ, the Father of glory, may give unto you the spirit of wisdom and revelation in the knowledge of him.

Ephesians 1:16-17

1

Why Do We
Need Revelation?

Unveiling the Life of Christ

For seventeen years I preached the gospel according to my evangelical, theological training without having a true understanding of the word *revelation*. I was a serious student of God's Word. My heart's desire was to know God. My research, notes and sermons, which I had carefully prepared according to my theological background, filled an entire filing cabinet. For one of my degrees in theology, I had written a dissertation on the five hundred cardinal doctrines of the church. I was a born-again Christian who was serving the Lord sincerely as a pastor and Bible college teacher. Yet, in spite of my study and training, I lived all those years without knowing God intimately. I did not know what it meant to receive divine revelation from the Word.

When I read the apostle Paul's prayer, "That I may know him [Christ]" (Phil. 3:10), I wondered why he would utter such a cry. It seemed to me that if anyone should have known Christ, it was Paul, whose many New Testament writings clearly revealed his intimate relationship with God. Why, then, would he cry out to know God with such an earnest plea?

After I began to know God through divine revelation, I understood that it was *because* Paul's heart was filled with personal revelation of God that he realized how much more there was to knowing God. Without divine revelation, I could not understand Paul's cry.

During my first years of ministry, I was not aware that I lacked revelation because I did not know that a personal, intimate relationship with God was possible. Though God had revealed Himself to me as my Savior and I had surrendered to His call on my life for ministry, my mind had not yet been touched by divine revelation. After God began His sovereign work of demolishing my incorrect theology, one of the first experiences I had of receiving revelation was related to true worship. Though I had conducted a choir and had had "worship services" in my church for years, I did not have a revelation of worship.

I had never seen people worshiping God in "spirit and in truth." There were no worship seminars during those years. One day in 1959 I was healed of a genetic bone disease that had taken the lives of several members of my family. That same day I was baptized in the Holy Spirit. Soon after the Holy Spirit took up residence inside me as my divine Teacher, I finally saw people truly worshiping God.

I observed true worship when I was invited to speak at a Pentecostal church. As I sat on the platform during the worship service, waiting to be introduced, I observed a young woman who was pouring out her heart to God in worship. I didn't know what she was doing, but as I watched, I saw her face become brighter and brighter, and I noticed tears rolling down her cheeks.

Although she was crying, I could tell she wasn't sad. She was telling God something, and I was determined to know what it was. I still had no theology to give me understanding of what she was doing because her behavior did not fit any of the five hundred cardinal doctrines I had studied.

Because I was the speaker for the service, I decided she would be courteous enough to answer my questions. So I descended from the platform, walked up to her and said, "Honey, you and the Lord are having a good time, aren't you?" She ignored me. Her lack of response seemed rude. I thought, *Doesn't she know I am the guest speaker?* She just continued to cry and speak to God. She acted as though she hadn't even heard me. She wasn't interested in me — she had her eyes on Someone else.

I returned to my seat on the platform and continued to observe her. She was "lost" in worship, oblivious to those around her. Though I did not understand what was happening at the time, I was fascinated by her expression of worship.

I decided to try again to make her hear me. I left the platform once more and stood behind her, repeating, "Honey, you and Jesus are having a good time, aren't you?" What I really wanted to ask her was, "What are you doing? What is this?" But she did not respond to me.

As I stood near her, I heard her say to the Lord, "I would rather hear Your voice than anyone else's on earth." I heard her tell Him she loved Him as tears streamed down her cheeks. The more she worshiped, the brighter her face shone.

I knew instinctively that this young woman was experiencing something wonderful, something that I had never experienced. But I didn't know what it was. Even with my great knowledge of theological terms, I couldn't define it, and that frustrated me. I didn't even have enough vocabulary to know how to ask the pastor what was happening to the girl. I went back and sat down, but I could not take my eyes off her — neither could I stay away from her.

For the third time, I walked down off the platform and approached her. Still, I received no satisfaction from this worshiper. She remained oblivious to my presence.

This time when I returned to the platform and sat down, I felt someone punch me. No one else was on the platform as far as I could see. But when I felt the punch, I heard the Holy Spirit say, "You can have that if you want it." I didn't even know what "that" was.

Personal Revelation of Worship

That night after the meeting was over, I went to the room where I was staying in a home in Decatur,

Georgia. I fell on my knees, and with tears streaming down my cheeks, I cried, "Father, what are you talking about? What is 'that' which I saw tonight?"

He said to me, "I seek a people who will worship Me in spirit and in truth."

"If that was worship," I asked, "then what have I been doing all these years?"

"Without this revelation of worship," He replied gently, "you have simply been having religious services."

Then the Lord asked me three simple questions. First He inquired, "What would you do if you had just heard the gates of heaven click behind your heels and you knew you were through with the devil forever?"

I responded vehemently, "You know I hate him!" I had spent months in the hospital as a patient, and I had followed behind casket after casket of family members who were being buried. I continued, "I would shout 'Glory!'"

He said, "Shout it."

I told Him that I would cry, "Hallelujah!"

He said, "Do it."

Then He asked me what I would do if I looked up and saw Jesus for the first time. I said that I would bow at His feet, kiss His nail-scarred hands and wash His feet with my tears. He said, "Do it."

I meditated on the efficacious, vicarious, substitutional, mediatorial work of Calvary, and suddenly I had a fresh glimpse of the Lamb of God. I began to bow before the Lamb who was slain, but He asked me to look up into His face. "When you see Me face to face," He asked, "what will you tell Me?"

When I heard those words, it was as if a dam within my soul broke, and torrents of praise flooded my lips. I told Him He was wonderful, and I recited the attributes of God I had learned in Bible college. I told Him He was omnipotent, omniscient, omnipresent, immutable, immaculate, emancipated, incarnate, divine. When I finished, He asked me if there was anything else I wanted to tell Him. With a sense of awe I responded simply, "You are wonderful."

A picture came to my mind, and I saw the face of Jesus before me as if it were framed. Then the frame faded. As I looked into His face, I told Him how much I loved Him. I had never done that in my life. I told Him how precious He was to me. I went on and on, trying to express my love for Him with my limited vocabulary.

While I was answering His three questions, it seemed as if just a few moments of time had passed. But it had actually been an hour and a half. For the first time in my life I had been in the presence of God in such a way that I had lost all consciousness of time. I had finally experienced true worship pouring out of my soul as I expressed my love and adoration for God. All my years of Bible training, study and ministry had not brought me to the place of worship that a few moments of divine revelation in His presence had done.

Since that time I have experienced the revelation of His presence through my praise and worship many times. And I have also learned to experience the glory of His presence as it is revealed through His precious Word.

Throughout history, God has been trying to reveal Himself to mankind. Long ago, He inspired men to write His Word — His love story — to us so that we could come to know Him. Because of the sin that separates us from God, we need revelation to be able to understand and grasp the true meaning of His Word and apply it to our lives. Intellectual studies alone will not unlock the truths of God's Word and bring understanding to our hearts.

What Is Revelation?

Revelation is absolutely necessary for us to enter into the type of relationship with God that He intended His children to enjoy. According to Webster's dictionary, the word *reveal* means "to unveil or make known through divine inspiration." When we speak of the revelation of Christ to believers, we are referring to the unveiling of the Christ who is inside us. Revelation does not make a believer into a son of God. A believer is made a child of God at the new birth and becomes a son as he grows to maturity.

A careful search of the Scriptures shows that Christ comes to live in our spirits when we are born again — when we accept the sacrifice of Christ's blood for the forgiveness of our sins. The apostle Peter declared that we were born again "not of corruptible seed, but of incorruptible, by the word of God, which liveth and abideth for ever" (1 Pet. 1:23). Christ is that incorruptible seed which lives in our spirits, giving us divine life when we are born again.

However, the divine life of Christ in our spirits must be revealed, or unveiled, to the soul — our minds, wills and emotions — in order for us to enjoy intimate relationship with God. For the unveiling to occur we must submit ourselves to a divine process of redemption that will bring us to a wonderful revelation of Christ in us, the hope of glory (Col. 1:27).

For seventeen years Christ lived inside me before I entered into the wonder of divine revelation — the unveiling of Christ's mind to my mind, His emotions to my emotions and His will to my will that transforms my character into Christlikeness. Though I lived according to a strict code of righteousness and holiness, I suffered terribly from a load of condemnation because I could not live up to that code.

Many sincere Christians who are genuinely born-again find themselves struggling to understand the Word and to walk in victory over sin and self because they have not entered into relationship with Christ through divine revelation.

The Necessity of Revelation

Revelation Motivates the Believer

Without revelation, we are not motivated by the love of Christ. Who is in charge of our affections, our thoughts, our plans? Whom do we put first — Christ? Or self, friends and the world? Do we follow Christ's teachings or man's opinions? How well do we know Christ? Is He really our life?

Paul the apostle described the struggle between the new creation and the natural mind, between Christ's nature and the nature of Adam, which lives in every believer (see Rom. 6–7). The old mind cannot know Christ, and the new mind cannot know Adam. However, when revelation comes, the law of life sets the believer free from the "law of Adam" (Rom. 8:2-4). Unless our minds are renewed by revelation of the Living Word, we will continually yield to the sinful desires of the flesh. We cannot be motivated by the love of Christ as long as our carnal nature is ruling us.

Revelation Reveals the Living Word

The apostle John knew Christ as the Living Word of God (John 1:1). As the Living Word, Christ lives in us and wants to unveil Himself to our minds, transforming our darkened thinking through His light. He does not just bring us information concerning the truth. That would only condemn us. Through revelation, Christ *becomes* truth to our hearts, manifesting Himself in our lives in that reality. Divine revelation is necessary if we are to know Christ as the Living Word.

Revelation Activates God's Eternal Purposes

Revelation is also necessary in order for us to walk in God's eternal purposes. The apostle Paul prayed for all the faithful in Christ Jesus, "That the God of our Lord Jesus Christ, the Father of glory, may give unto you the spirit of wisdom and revelation in the knowledge of him" (Eph. 1:17). Paul says that only when we have this spirit can we know the hope of His calling.

We must enter into unity with God's will for our lives through divine revelation. Christ wants our *minds* to think His thoughts, our *emotions* to express His love and our *wills* to choose to allow His will to be performed in and through us. Such unity can only happen as we cultivate our relationship with Christ and become one with His eternal purposes through divine revelation.

Paul described the wonderful relationship in Christ

which divine revelation makes possible when he wrote:

> I am crucified with Christ: nevertheless I live; yet not I, but Christ liveth in me: and the life which I now live in the flesh I live by the faith of the Son of God, who loved me, and gave himself for me (Gal. 2:20).

Before the Living Word can be revealed to us, in us and through us, we must realize that we are destitute of divine life without Him. Even knowledge *about* Him cannot give us life. We need to understand how hopeless our plight was before we were born again.

Understanding the Plight of Mankind

When God made mankind, He did not intend for man to have three distinct parts — spirit, soul and body. He created him as a living soul in a perfect body. God, who is a Spirit (John 4:24), communed with man Spirit to spirit. He was able to talk with Adam and fellowship with him through Adam's spirit to his soul. Nothing hindered this divine communion and fellowship. What delight must have filled Adam and his wife as they walked with God in the garden of Eden, enjoying spiritual communion with God!

When sin entered, what God had warned would happen did occur — the spirits of Adam and Eve died to their relationship with God. A "veil of flesh" dropped inside them, between soul and spirit, placing the mind, will and emotions of man in charge and cutting off communication with God. Their flesh separated them from communion with God much like the veil in Moses' tabernacle separated man from the holy of holies where the presence of God was manifested. Though Adam and Eve did not die a physical death immediately (God had never planned for them to die physically), they could no longer commune with God, Spirit to spirit. Their souls now ruled them independently from God. They had died, as God had warned them they would, to their relationship with their Creator.

All men born in Adam are born with a dead spirit. Because our dead spirits do not have the capacity to relate to God, our souls, which are under the dominion of disobedience and sin, rule us. We are born with rebellious wills, carnal minds and warped emotions.

The Scriptures teach clearly that the carnal mind is an enemy of God and that those who are ruled by it will experience death (Rom. 8). The carnal mind is blinded, vain in its imaginations. It produces unspiritual thoughts and is inflated with a sense of self-importance (Col. 2:18). Because of the disposition of the carnal mind, the Scriptures exhort believers to "be renewed in the spirit of your mind" (Eph. 4:23) and to "let this mind be in you which was also in Christ Jesus" (Phil. 2:5).

Even after we are born again and have the life of Christ living in our spirits, we cannot hope to understand spiritual life with our carnal minds. The Scriptures declare, "But the natural man receiveth not the things of the Spirit of God: for they are foolishness unto him: neither can he know them, because they are spiritually discerned" (1 Cor. 2:14).

Accepting Jesus as our Savior causes the seed of life in Christ to be planted in our spirits by the Holy Spirit. In this supernatural experience we are given the gift of eternal life. Jesus said, "And this is life eternal, that they might know thee the only true God, and Jesus Christ, whom thou hast sent" (John 17:3). To have Christ living in our spirits is to enter into eternal life in God.

It is important for us to realize that the Spirit of Christ lives in us once we are born again. Yet if we do not go beyond the mere recognition of His indwelling presence, we will never truly know Christ.

As believers, we know about Christ's benefits, His gifts and what He did for us on Calvary. But how intimately do we know *Him?* To know Christ is to have a relationship with Him that allows Him to work in us God's original purpose for creating mankind. That purpose is for God to commune and fellowship with us, sharing His great heart of love with His family. He wants to pour His divine life into us and make us mature sons in His character.

Though Adam was created in the image of God, he did not have God's character. Divine character is formed through right choices that result in obedience to God. God does not want robots who love Him because they are programmed to do so. He wants mankind to choose to love Him, for choice is the essence of love. When Adam and his wife chose to disobey God, they rejected the love and purpose God had for mankind.

Christ, the second Adam, came to fulfill the purpose of God for man, living in perfect obedience to His Father. At Calvary He suffered the penalty for mankind's disobedience and made possible our reconciliation to God. Through redemption, we can once again choose to love God and obey Him, allowing His character to be formed in us so we become sons and daughters of God with knowledge. For our relationship with Him to become all that it was meant to be, we must allow a divine process of removing the veil of flesh that separates us from Him.

The Veil of Flesh

As we have mentioned, when mankind fell and lost relationship with God, a veil of flesh fell between the soul and the spirit, separating us from God. God demonstrated in "type" the separation we experience within our own beings because of the veil when He gave Moses the design for the tabernacle. He required that the holy of holies, the place where God manifested His presence, be separated from the holy place by a thick veil.

Man's access to God's awesome presence was extremely limited. Only a representative of the people, the high priest, could enter the holy of holies, and he could go only once a year, after a strict code of righteousness that God had prescribed was followed exactly. Otherwise, he would die.

God knew that His chosen people would tell Moses that they did not want to hear from God for themselves. He knew they would want Moses to go and find out what He said and then tell them. So the great, omnipotent God condescended to meet with man one day a year on the Day of Atonement. The ark was placed behind a veil in the tabernacle, and no one was to go beyond the veil except the high priest on that one day.

In the temple that existed in Jesus' time, that veil of separation still hung. But on the terrible day when the Son of God was crucified, the veil was torn in two from top to bottom. Have we realized the significance of the ripping open of the veil? It symbolizes for us the destruction of the veil in our temples — our flesh — so that we can have unlimited access to God, and He to us.

The apostle Paul declared, "Know ye not that ye are the temple of God?" (1 Cor. 3:16). God's purpose in ordaining temples is to fill them with His glory. Every tabernacle and temple in the Old Testament was constructed for the purpose of being filled with the glorious presence of God. The natural veils that hung in them represented, in type, the veil of flesh that separates the life of God living in our spirits from the natural life of our souls.

Being born again is having the incorruptible seed of the life of God placed in our spirits. This experience gives us eternal life and places us within the family of God. However, only the rending of the veil of flesh can bring the wonderful revelation of the life of Christ to our souls, transforming our character and bringing us into intimate relationship with God. Only as the veil is removed can Christ be manifested to the world in all His love.

Rending the Veil

When God made man He did not intend to have His presence shut away in a box — the ark of the covenant — or to have a priest come into His presence only on one day a year. God made man to walk and fellowship with Him just as Adam did before Adam's disobedience. God wanted to walk with man and pour Himself into him when his will was not rebellious and his mind was not carnal.

Adam and Eve were able to commune with God freely. They knew nothing about humanism until they touched the tree of the knowledge of good and evil and became as gods in charge of their own lives. Before their act of betrayal, their inner sanctuaries were wide open, vacuums for God to pour Himself into and to fill with His glory.

When man chose to disobey the command of God, he died to his relationship with God and could no longer commune with Him. Calvary, God's divine remedy, was required so that man could be redeemed back to God. Once we accept the sacrifice of Christ and are born again, a hidden Person lives in our inner sanctuary, our spirits. But many believers do not know Him very well. We may have peace with God and know something of His eternal benefits for our souls, but we do not know Him intimately.

The revelation of Christ brings the rending of the veil of flesh between our souls and our spirits, which allows us to know the wonders of His Person. We see Him as He is: the Exalted One, the Brightness of God's glory, the Express Image of His Person, the King of glory, the Pearl of great price, the Rock in a weary land, the Cup that runneth over, the Rod and Staff, the Father to the orphan, the Husband to the widow, the Bright and Morning Star, the Lily of the Valley, the Rose of Sharon, the Honey in the rock, the Passover Lamb, the Captain of our salvation, the Mighty to save, the Messenger of beautiful feet, the Avenger of God's elect, the Justifier, the Sanctifier. These are only a few of the biblical descriptions of His Person. This Christ cannot be seen with the eye, touched with the hand or heard with the ear of the natural man.

Since the Scriptures declare that no flesh can know Christ (1 Cor. 2:9-16), how do we come to know Him intimately and personally? Is God a tease? Does He tantalize us with a wonderful reality that we cannot realize? The Scriptures clearly show that God intends for His children to know Him in all of His beauty. The Scriptures themselves reveal to us how this is possible.

The Divine Knife

The Scriptures declare that the Word of God is sharper than a two-edged sword, dividing asunder the soul and the spirit (Heb. 4:12). The dividing doesn't happen out in the atmosphere somewhere — it happens inside us. It is a work of the infinite, blessed, omnipotent, omniscient, omnipresent, Third Person of the Godhead.

The Scriptures teach that the Holy Spirit came to take the things of Jesus and show them to us (John 16:15). He came to reveal Jesus in us and to fill our temples with God. In order to do that He has a divine mandate to split open the veil between our soul and spirit so that the life of Jesus can be manifest in our lives.

When the divine rending releases divine life from our spirit to our soul, Christ's mind becomes our mind, His will our will, His emotions our emotions. The Holy Spirit has purposed to clean up the whole house to reveal Jesus — to unveil Jesus in us. As we fill our minds with the Word of God and yield to the revelatory work of the Holy Spirit in us, He will precipitate the destruction of the veil of flesh within us.

How many of us have experienced this rending

work of the Holy Spirit in one area of our lives and have felt its wonderful cleansing power only to discover that the Holy Spirit is now shining His light on another strength in our flesh that has not submitted to the Lordship of Christ? To the degree that we yield to the process of the rending of our flesh, allowing the Word of God to do its work of "penetrating to the dividing line of the breath of life [soul] and the immortal spirit, and of joints and marrow [that is, of the deepest parts of our nature], exposing and sifting and analyzing and judging the very thoughts and purposes of the heart" (Heb. 4:12, AMP), to that degree we will become like Christ. The life of Christ can be revealed *through* us only after He is revealed *in* us.

It was many years after my salvation experience before I understood that when Jesus Himself baptized me in the Holy Spirit, He moved into my spirit with the intent to split open the veil between my soul and my spirit so He could reveal Himself in me. It is imperative to be filled with the Holy Spirit in order to receive divine revelation.

Yet even many who consider themselves Spirit-filled Christians are not yet walking in the life-changing revelation of the Christ-life within them. They do not have an intimate relationship with Christ. That is because they have not submitted to the process involved in the tearing open of the veil of flesh that separates His divine life in their spirits from their minds, emotions and wills.

The divine life of Christ stayed locked up inside me for seventeen years before I had the first experience of knowing what it meant to have that veil of flesh ripped open and to have divine revelation come to my mind. In the years since then I have continued to

23

submit to the process of having the Christ-life revealed in me. Christ has become the Lover of my soul. He is my Bridegroom. The lovely Person of Christ fascinates me. I am no longer seeking just His blessings or benefits, but His Person.

To come to know Christ intimately in this way, I have had to experience the rending of the veil of flesh between my spirit, where He resides, and my soul, which is still under the influence of sin and carnality.

During my years of seminary training I sat under every Bible teacher they would let me sit under. I begged for classes. I wanted to take everything they taught about the Bible. I wanted to be a person who rightly divided the Book. I wanted to be an exegetical theologian, an expositor of the Word. I started out with a hunger for God and His Word. For seventeen years I taught the Word and studied it to know God. Though I did not know God by revelation during those years, the Holy Spirit prepared me through my studies for the day when I would begin to know Him, when all that information would start coming alive in me.

I will never forget the first night that the Holy Spirit began to "divide asunder" the veil of flesh between my soul and my spirit and I began to see Jesus — the Wonderful One my teachers had told me about but could not show me. No one can show us Jesus except the Holy Spirit. That is His divine mandate — to reveal Jesus to us. As you will see in the following chapters, it took some extreme circumstances in my life to bring me to the place where the Holy Spirit could begin to reveal Jesus in me.

To the glory of God, I have a testimony that the

Holy Spirit is able to pierce the thickest veil of theology, doctrine and prejudice in order to reveal Jesus to one who thought she knew God but who, in reality, needed desperately for Him to be revealed to her.

Revelation is not a theory or a doctrine to me but a living reality that saved me from an early death. Miraculously, revelation brought to me the life of Christ in His resurrection power to set me on the path of divine discovery that I am still walking today.

Jesus saith unto him...If ye had known me, ye should have known my Father also.

John 14:6-7

2

Relationship Through Revelation

My Personal Journey to Revelation

Is anything more sorrowful recorded as coming from Jesus' lips than the question He asked His disciples, "Have I been so long time with you, and yet hast thou not known me?" (John 14:9). Why did Jesus perform miracles? Why did He teach the multitudes the truths of the kingdom? Jesus said it was to reveal the heavenly Father to us (John 14:9). He said He did only those things He saw the Father doing (John 5:19). And when the disciples asked Jesus to teach them to pray, He began by wrapping all the names of God that had been revealed through the Old Testament into one: "Our Father."

Yet Jesus' disciples walked with Him daily for over three years and never knew Him. They followed Him, saw His miracles and heard His teachings. They felt a certain affection for Him. But their understanding was limited to the natural world. They knew Jesus as a man — one with phenomenal powers — but still a man. They did not recognize that they were walking with God.

Although Peter did receive the revelation that Jesus was the Christ, a moment later he was rebuking Jesus for telling them about His death to come. Jesus had to correct Peter sharply.

It seems by Jesus' question that even He marveled at their inability to grasp spiritual realities. Was it possible that He had been with them so long, revealing all the while the love of the Father, and that they still did not know Him?

Unfortunately, many Christians today face the same dilemma the disciples did. They have received Christ as their Savior and are following Him and His teachings, but they do not have divine revelation of who He is, the Christ who lives inside of them.

I can relate to the disciples as well as to sincere Christians who have not yet entered into relationship with Christ through divine revelation. I was rocked in a Methodist cradle, reared in a Methodist home. I grew up in a very honest, good, moral home. Though I went to church from the time I was a baby, I didn't know anything about being born again.

Even as a young woman, I didn't know Jesus as my Savior. I went to church and Sunday school and sang in the choir. I was the youngest girl ever invited to represent the women's missionary society of the United Methodist Church (M.E. Church South then). I stood in that position at Brevard College as a nine-year-old and again as a thirteen-year-old, the youngest girl ever selected.

Longing for Relationship

I remember wanting to know God from the time I was a little girl. I used to go out and look up at the stars or watch the clouds. I was filled with awe and wondered if I would ever know the One who made them. I grew up in the church and married very young, right after I finished high school. I had been on my way to study at Brevard College to teach in the Methodist faith when I fell in love with a handsome young man. I proceeded to date him and persuaded my parents to give me permission to marry. At not quite seventeen, instead of attending college, I married George Parrish. One year later, we had a baby boy, Darrell.

During this time I met a Presbyterian girl who worked in the same office I worked in. That Presbyterian girl knew Jesus. She had a relationship with the Lord such as I had never seen before. She didn't preach at me, but her life nagged me. I couldn't stand to be with her, and I couldn't stand to be away from her. I wanted to be near her so that what she had would rub off on me. But every time I got around her I felt convicted of my sin, though I did not understand then that conviction was what I was feeling.

She was praying for me, and she had Methodist

and Presbyterian people in a Bible class praying for me. She knew I didn't know Jesus even though I was a Sunday school and VBS teacher, a member of the choir and a faithful church-goer. Who didn't think I was going to heaven? But when I met this Presbyterian girl, suddenly by the law of contrast I saw myself in a different light.

My Presbyterian friend didn't talk to me about my soul. She would just tell me about the good time they had had at the prayer meeting the night before and about how precious Jesus was to her. She would talk about Jesus as if He were her sweetheart. It sounded like blasphemy to me. After all, wasn't God austere? Weren't we to be afraid of Him? Wasn't it irreverent to talk about Jesus as this girl did?

But she knew God in a way I had never known Him. I began to get so disturbed I couldn't sleep. I would awaken my husband and ask, "Honey, if I died before morning, would I go to heaven?" He would always answer me, "That is the reason I married you, Fuchsia. You were a good girl. Yes, you would go to heaven."

That was all he knew, but someone else was telling me differently. The Third Person of the infinite Godhead became a companion in my room at night, trying to reveal Jesus to my darkened soul.

Old hymns that I had sung all my life in the Methodist church began echoing in the corridors of my spirit. I remember hearing the words, "And He walks with me, and He talks with me, and He tells me I am His own; And the joy we share as we tarry there none other has ever known. He speaks, and the sound of His voice is so sweet the birds hush their singing."[1]

As those words floated through my mind, I realized

suddenly that either I was singing a lie or someone had written a fantasy. I did not know I was His own, and I had not heard Him talk to me. In those night hours the Holy Spirit began to address eternal values in my soul.

It Is Well With My Soul

A citywide revival was planned for my town in which all the churches participated. They did it for the sake of unity, not for the salvation of souls. They didn't preach about being born again. They had agreed not to preach doctrinal messages because of the different denominations represented. They called on people from various churches to sing.

At that time I could sing, but I didn't have a song in my heart. However, I was selected to be one of the singers for the revival, as was a friend of the Presbyterian girl who was fervently praying for my salvation. We were to sing a duet. Since I sang alto and "It Is Well With My Soul" has a beautiful alto part, I suggested we sing that.

That night when we sang, I got through the first stanza of the song pretty well. By the second stanza my voice was faltering. During the third stanza tears were in my eyes. Nothing had happened to my throat, but I could not sing any longer because for the first time in my life, I realized it was *not* well with my soul. I wanted somebody to tell me what was wrong, to tell me that I could know Jesus. I needed to know *how* to make it well with my soul. People applauded our performance of the song, but no one told me what I needed to know before I left the meeting that night.

When I got home, I went to my bedroom and

opened the dresser drawer to take out my nightgown. Suddenly, I fell to my knees under a terrible power of conviction. Revelation of my need for a Savior had come to my heart.

The Holy Ghost came to my spirit and told me I could know that what I had been singing was real. I cried, "O God, if there is such a thing as *knowing* what I have been simply *singing* about in church for years, tell me tonight. Let me know that I am ready to go to heaven. Let me know that I am a child of God."

In just a few moments, like a bolt of lightning, an old-fashioned Methodist salvation experience struck my inner man, and I was born again. I knew that I had been "translated into the kingdom of his dear son" (Col. 1:13), and the melody of heaven became the anthem of my spirit. Sovereignly, God had come to save this Methodist girl. He had heard the prayers of my Presbyterian friend and of those she had asked to pray for me.

That night I began to sing, and I have never stopped since. I knew I had passed from death to life. and I wouldn't have given an angel in heaven a nickel to tell me I had been born again. I didn't know what to call it. I didn't know whether it was regeneration, conversion, or being born again — I just knew it was real.

I jumped up off my knees and looked at my husband, who had been standing there and had witnessed what had happened, and I said, "Honey, I am all right with God. Something has happened to me. There is nothing between my soul and my Savior." I had moved out of darkness into light, and I knew that it was well with my soul. I thought everyone in the world wanted to know it. I stopped everyone I saw on the street to tell them about my experience. I testified to everyone I knew and to those I didn't know.

Called to Preach and Teach

A little over a year later, I had another sovereign visitation from God. I was in my room waiting for George to come home from work. As I lay in bed, I heard a voice call my name louder than a person's voice. I raised up in the bed and answered it questioningly. "Yes?" As I sat there for a moment, I sensed that my room was filled with the presence of God. No one answered my response so I lay back down.

A few moments later I was awakened, and I heard that voice call my name again. I sat up and decided it must be the people who were living upstairs in our house. I got up and looked up the stairwell, but I did not hear a sound. There was no one in the house. I went back and lay down on my bed. The third time I heard my name called aloud, I fell by my bedside trembling. I asked, "God, is this You?"

He said, "Yes, Fuchsia. I want you to preach and teach My Word."

One of the greatest blessings in my heritage is that my parents taught me to obey them. My daddy, the best friend I ever had on earth, taught me to obey and to love to please him. So when the infinite, almighty, eternal, triune God — my heavenly Father — walked into my room, called me by name and told me He wanted me to preach and teach His Word, I didn't question whether I had an option to obey Him or not. My earthly daddy had taught me unconditional obedience.

I knew I had heard the voice of God, and no one could tell me I could not preach because I was a woman. I did not think that some committee or board needed to determine according to their theology whether I could or should feed His sheep as He had asked me to do.

I surrendered that night to God, although I didn't know how or when or where I would fulfill the mandate He placed on my life. I was a wife and young mother. It did not seem likely that I could get the preparation I would need to preach the gospel. But God always provides where He has commanded an obedient heart.

My husband was a petty officer in the Navy during the latter part of the Korean war. He was called back to active duty, and I was able to enter Bible college as God sovereignly opened the door. God sat me down in Bible school at John Wesley College in Greensboro, North Carolina, while my husband was away in the military and my boy was little.

After graduation, God led me out into the ministry, opening doors for me to preach the Word. I had never heard of a woman preacher. My mother was so distressed at the prospect of my preaching that she wore black and cried and said that her daughter was dead. But I knew I had heard from God, and I could not be deterred. (In later years, happily, I became my mother and father's pastor. After my father's death, my mother became one of my greatest supporters.)

God had sovereignly revealed Himself to me as Savior and Lord and had called me into the ministry. He opened the way for me to attend Bible college and do graduate work at the University of North Carolina. I knew I was called to preach His Word, though that was more unusual for a woman in that time than it is now. Yet He opened doors across the country for meetings.

My first husband, who is now in heaven, was saved in our home one week after he witnessed my dramatic conversion experience. He became a wonderful soloist and sang in our meetings. Later when we pastored, he led the music and directed the choir as well. We worked in the kingdom together as a team, walking happily together in ministry. We were sincere believers, living according to the understanding we had from our training in the Word. But God put us on a painful path that brought us to a place of revelation we never knew existed.

Surrounded by Tragedy

During those years tragedy came to our family. My parents lost two sons to a genetic bone disease. Not long after I started pastoring, my brother who was still living came to our church with his son. He told me that his son was showing some alarming symptoms which indicated the onset of the same illness. For months we watched the child slowly die. By now all the boys in my family were gone except my own son and my one remaining brother.

Then my daddy became ill. I watched this great man, a member of my church board who had walked with God and was so devout — my "papa" — waste away. All I could do was stand helplessly by, not knowing why these things had to be.

Then one day, during the last stages of my daddy's illness, my body, too, began to register frightening signs of illness. I felt instinctively that my days of ministry would soon be over. I returned home to spend some time with my daddy before his death. We had a most providential conversation during one day of my visit. I had been my daddy's pastor for nine years, and we enjoyed sharing from the Word together. But that day, he walked into the room where I sat with his face showing great pain and with his Bible in his hand.

He looked at me and said, "Daughter, I think we have missed something, haven't we?"

"Why, Daddy?" I questioned.

"I keep reading about Elijah. Elijah knew a God I don't think we know in our day." He looked me straight in the face and shot out his question, "Pastor, where is the God of Elijah?"

I carefully explained to him as I had been taught concerning healing and miracles. I said gently, "Daddy, we don't need that now because the Scriptures teach that when that which is perfect is come, these gifts will be done away with. Jesus is that perfect One who has come, so we don't need miracles and healing anymore. We have the written Word: the Word has come." That was the last cogent conversation I ever had with my daddy.

I had gone home to help my mother take care of Daddy. But I began to hurt so intensely that I said regretfully to my sister-in-law, "Don't tell my mother why, but I am not going to be able to stay until the weekend. I am suffering so badly that I must go home to see my doctor. Please don't tell Mother. She has enough with Daddy." Without explaining why, I told Mother that I was going home.

Saturday morning I went to my study with every bone of my body feeling as if it were breaking, especially in my spine. When I got into my study, a pain hit the base of my neck, went down my spine, shot into both of my legs and seemed to jerk my backbone. I fell to the floor and cried in pain. Then I struggled to my feet and went out the door screaming for help. I didn't know where I was.

My husband and friends found me, picked me up and carried me to my bed. I was not aware of my surroundings until the following Tuesday. As I lay there, I became aware of my husband sitting at the foot of my bed. He was talking to a Nazarene preacher.

I heard him ask, "Why? Can you tell me why this woman, who loves God with all her heart and has studied His Word all her life to be able to train men and women in the gospel message has to suffer this?" My first thought was that he sounded bitter. I said, "Honey, it is all right. Don't worry."

They wheeled me into a hospital in North Carolina where my testimony is documented in their files. They put me in traction and packed sand bags around my body. They gave me cortisone and many different kinds of shots to relieve my pain. Prior to my admittance, I had written out my funeral arrangements, picked out my pallbearers and purchased a cemetery lot. My tombstone was erected in the Overlook Cemetery in Eden, North Carolina. The only things missing were a date of death on the tombstone and a body in the lot.

One afternoon shortly after my husband left my hospital room, I heard him coming back down the hall. He had been gone only a few minutes, and I knew it wasn't time for him to return. Yet I recognized his step coming toward my room. As he approached the door to my room, he said, "Honey?"

I said, "Yes, dear, come in." My head was strapped in braces as it lay on the pillow, and I was lying between sandbags. I said, "You are back soon. Come over where I can see you."

As soon as he came into the room, I knew something was wrong. I saw that someone was behind him. The nurse put a shot in my arm, a precautionary measure the doctor was taking. He had said to my husband, "It will be hard for her to bear this news." He knew that my daddy was one of the dearest people on earth to me.

George said, "Honey, I bring you bad news. Papa is dead. He left today." I began to weep.

In spite of my physical condition, I determined to go to my daddy's funeral. The nurses packed a stretcher carefully to make sure it would not hurt me. They carried me to an ambulance and drove me sixty miles to my parents' home. I rode to the cemetery in an ambulance behind my daddy.

It was the sixth time I had heard a preacher say "ashes to ashes and dust to dust" when burying a precious member of my family. I didn't ever want to hear those words again. I asked them not to lower my daddy into the grave in my presence. They placed him on the mound of dirt covered with green turf.

As the ambulance I was in turned around, I looked out the back window and said, "Good-bye, Papa. I will be with you in a few months." I felt that I would be with him soon. I was ready to meet God. I was paid up, prayed up, packed up and ready to go up. I had preached seventeen years for Him, pastoring and teaching. I had carried the gospel to many people; I had taught Bible school students; I had preached in camp meetings. I knew I was ready to go to heaven.

One day, several weeks after my daddy's funeral, the doctor walked into my hospital room and said, "Fuchsia, we are going to fasten you into a brace at the base of your neck and let you go home for a few weeks. Then we will bring you in and fuse your back together to keep you from hemorrhaging." The nurses fitted me with the brace, and I went home.

A Miraculous Intervention

I had been home a few days when I received word that a teachers' meeting for many of the friends with whom I had taught was scheduled for the following Sunday morning. I had a friend call the doctor to ask if I could be carried to the service. The doctor said I could. I took medicine for the pain, and my friend drove me sixty miles to the service, which I assumed would be my last.

The church where the meeting was to be held was not one I would have chosen to attend. It was the First Pentecostal Holiness Church of Danville, Virginia. I was going only because the teachers I had worked with were going to be there that morning. It was one of those churches I considered strange. Over six hundred people attended the Pentecostal church the morning I went.

I was now a college professor. I had been teaching and pastoring as well as doing radio work. I considered myself to be intelligent. And I loved God with all my heart. I believed in commitment, consecration and holiness. Yet, as a result of my choice to attend a strange service, I was carried to a church with which I did not agree doctrinally or experientially.

I learned later that at 4:00 A.M. on that Sunday

morning God had awakened the seventy-year-old retired superintendent of the Pentecostal Holiness Church, who was to be the guest speaker that morning in the church he had formerly pastored, and told him to preach a certain message. God had arranged to move the current pastor of the church out of the pulpit. (I told the pastor later that if he had been preaching that morning, I would be dead. He had learned how to "have church." His church was becoming dignified and socially acceptable — not too many displays of emotion or speaking in tongues. Everything was done by the clock so that he could dismiss his congregation at noon sharp.)

Though the church had lost its former revival spirit, a prayer group of about seventy-five godly people met every Monday night in the basement of the church to ask God for revival. In that prayer group was one of my former students, who was also one of the teachers with whom I was meeting that morning.

She had been asking the group to pray for my healing. She called my next-door neighbor, a Lutheran woman, every week to see how I was doing. Every week my neighbor would tell her, "She is worse." And Edna would respond, "Praise the Lord." My Lutheran neighbor thought Edna was strange.

When I was carried into the church that Sunday morning, the prayer group was ecstatic because they knew that the stage had been set for God to do a miracle.

I had said to my friend who drove me to the church, "If nothing else is accomplished this morning, I want you to bring Edna to me. Before I leave this world, I would like to get her straightened out. She has gotten into that strange church and is mixed up. I really want her saved from that." I did not know that it was not Edna — but me — who was going to be straightened out that day.

During the service, the guest speaker preached the message God had awakened him to tell him to preach. He had argued with God, telling Him that he had already preached that sermon to this church when he pastored it. God simply said to him, "You preach; I keep the records."

He began his sermon with deep conviction and fervency, declaring to us the reality of the God of Elijah. My thoughts raced back to my last conversation with my daddy. I found myself gripped by this godly preacher's words. Suddenly he moved from behind the pulpit, stood beside it and looked me straight in the eye. He said, "My beloved, you may have followed the dearest one on earth to you and left him on a green mound. But he didn't take his God away from you. He wants you to know that the God of Elijah is in this church today, and He is the same today as He has always been." I felt my daddy had gotten to heaven and told God he had a dumb daughter down on earth who needed to know that the God of Elijah is alive today.

I was stunned. I felt as if somebody had punched me in the ribs. I knew who it was, because I had been talking to Him for seventeen years. He was my Savior. He told me to go forward for prayer, but I quickly dismissed the thought as impossible. I couldn't even stand up. The preacher started to close the service but then paused to say, "I feel strangely led to sing an old Methodist hymn. Do you know that old Methodist hymn, 'Majestic Sweetness Sits Enthroned'?"

The song leader replied, "Yes, we do. Let's take out our songbooks." So the congregation of the First Pentecostal Church sang a Methodist hymn to this Methodist pastor who was sitting there in pain with her funeral arrangements already made.

Again I felt the Holy Spirit say, "Go forward for prayer." I responded, "There is no altar call. How am I going to get up there?" The church continued with another stanza, "He saw me plunged in deep distress and flew to my relief." Again I heard Him say, "Go forward for prayer."

About that time they were ready to finish the song, and I prayed, "God, if this is you, make them sing another stanza." They finished the song and closed their books. But the speaker got up and said, "Isn't there another stanza to that song?"

"Yes, there is," the song leader replied.

"Could we sing it, please?" the speaker asked. So they sang it.

I pulled on the girl's dress who had taken me to the church and said, "Stand me up." She looked at me strangely but heard my tone and knew she dared not fail to respond. So she manipulated my braces and stood me up. Dragging my weakened body in my braces I picked up my Bible, went up to the little man, looked into his face and said, "Sir, I don't know why I am here. But I have a feeling that God would like these people to pray for me."

He said, "All right." He reached into the pulpit and got a small bottle out. Then he greased me and prayed, "In the name of Jesus" like I had never heard it said before. It changed my life — and my theology — totally. Suddenly my eyes were on Jesus, and I had a foretaste of the glory that is yet to be revealed in the church when Jesus stands in our midst.

Nothing dramatic happened in my body when he prayed. God simply spoke to me about my consecration. He asked me to surrender to Him the same way I had the night He had called me to preach. I did. In my limited understanding I believed that I had just been anointed for my burial. Dragging myself in my braces, I started to return to my seat.

When I reached my chair at the seventh pew, suddenly I heard a voice thunder, "If you will be willing and obedient, you shall eat the good of the land" (Is. 1:19). In an instant, the words "of the land" stood up like neon lights before my eyes.

I stood as if frozen and looked at those words — "of the land." I realized at that moment that they didn't refer to heaven. Eating the good of the land meant right here and now. I grabbed that understanding by faith. I had a witness in the spirit that I was going to live, though I didn't yet know that I was going to be healed.

Then I heard the Lord ask me, "Are you willing to be identified with these people — to be one of them?"

Before I had time to bring my theology to argue against Him, I said, "Yes, Lord." Then I turned and looked at the man who had preached that morning, and asked, "Sir, may I say something?"

He said, "Of course. Testimonies are always in order in this church."

"I am going to live. Jesus just told me so." I held my Bible and stood there in tears, still in my braces, thinking that that was how I would have to preach the gospel.

I turned again and started to my seat. Suddenly the

power of God struck the base of my neck, went down my spine and coursed through my body. The miraculous, healing power of God put me back together instantly. It was the infinite, triune, omnipotent God who touched me that morning. And when He turned me loose, I ran and danced and shouted. I had been struck by resurrection power, which healed me and set me free.

One hour and twenty minutes later — same service, same people — over three hundred of the six hundred people present had been visited by the Holy Spirit. God had brought revival in answer to the prayers of those who had prayed every Monday night for almost a year for revival and for my healing.

That morning I ran the aisles when I didn't believe in it. I had my hands up, though I had never raised them in praise before. I shouted, and the other people shouted. I finally ended up in the corner. They said I danced and shouted, "I don't hurt." Then I started to take off my braces. Previously I had suffered worse pain with my deteriorating bones than I thought it was possible for a human being to suffer.

Finally, there I was, standing in the corner of the church with my hands up, having exhausted myself in gratitude for this unexpected miracle. I heard myself saying, "Bless the Lord, O my soul, and all that is within me, bless His holy name." As I was standing there facing the wall with tears of joy rolling down my cheeks, trying to thank Him, my soul began to bless Him in a language that I had never learned or heard before. Not only was I healed from the top of my head to the tips of my toes; I was filled with the Holy Ghost.

I drove my own automobile sixty miles home that

day. On the way I stopped at my mother's house. I went running in to tell her the good news, and she almost fainted when she saw me. The following Tuesday I went to see my doctor. As I walked into the office unassisted and without braces, I told the nurse not to say a word to the doctor. I jumped up backwards onto the examining table and sat there smiling. The nurse was dismayed at my actions and cried out for me to be careful. She left the room to call the doctor.

He was a Baptist lay preacher. When he had examined me thoroughly and taken x-rays and done blood work, he looked at me and said, "Fuchsia, this is a miracle. Jump down from there, girl." I jumped down, and he put his arm around my waist. We walked out into the reception area to a room full of people and he said to the receptionist, "Strike her name out of our book. She has been on a doctor's book since she was eighteen years old. The only thing she will need now is some vitamins, because I have a feeling she is not going to stop wherever she goes." Then he turned to the people in the waiting room and said, "This is what faith will do." He pronounced me completely healed.

More Wonderful Than Healing

I knew that I would not have lived more than a few months if God had not miraculously intervened in my life and healed my body. That was almost forty years ago, and I have enjoyed the results of the miracle all these years. Yet something more wonderful than physical healing happened to me that Sunday morning. Within a few days after my healing, I realized that the baptism of the Holy Spirit I had received that day had ushered me into a new relationship with God.

My divine Teacher had come to fill me with Himself and to split open the veil between my soul and my spirit. He intervened in my desperate circumstances and healed me miraculously when my mind did not believe the doctrine of healing. For the first time in my life I began to understand through revelation the same scriptures I had studied and taught faithfully for many years. They came alive to me, not as information, but as power that was working in me and transforming my life.

All my theology and knowledge of the Word had been challenged by the healing I had received and by the baptism of the Holy Spirit I had experienced. I pondered, "If I was so wrong in my understanding of those things, what else is mistaken in my theology?" My Teacher, the blessed Holy Spirit, the Third Person of the Godhead, came to set up His classroom in my spirit. He let me know that His classroom was always open. It was not like mine, which ran for sixty or ninety minutes at a time. I could ask any questions I wanted to, any time of the day or night. He would be there to help me understand what He really meant when He wrote the Book.

I was keenly aware that my intellect had not been able to grasp the reality of an omnipotent God in spite of all my years of study. I was entering a spiritual adventure in which I was like a little child, sitting at the feet of my Teacher and asking Him to teach me. For the next five years, I did not go to bed more than two or three nights a week. I studied the Scriptures, and the Holy Spirit gave me understanding on how they fit together. I would look up all the references on a single word, discovering how that word fit from the Old Testament to the New Testament.

As the Word of God came alive to me, the Holy Spirit wrote it on the tablet of my heart. From Leviticus to Hebrews and from Joshua to Ephesians, I began to see that the Bible was more than just the Logos (written) Word of God. It was Christ, the Living Word, who was becoming my life.

Nothing is ever wasted in God. Those seventeen years I had studied and prayed over the Word and preached the good news to people had prepared me for the wonderful revelation of God that I experienced after receiving the baptism of the Holy Spirit. The Word of God is the basis for all divine revelation, and knowledge of the Word increases our capacity for receiving that revelation of Christ. Though my knowledge of the Word proved faulty in the light of the Holy Spirit, He was able to use it as a point of reference to show me the truth of what He really meant.

In order that we might understand the basis of all divine revelation, it is important that we consider and understand the authority of the Scriptures.

All scripture is given by inspiration of God, and is profitable for doctrine, for reproof, for correction, for instruction in righteousness: That the man of God may be perfect, thoroughly furnished unto all good works.

2 Timothy 3:16-17

3

The Basis of
All True Revelation

The Authority of the Scriptures

We dare not say we have received revelation apart from the written Word of God. To do so opens us to error and outright deception of the enemy. God's Word is truth, and we must always carefully compare scripture with scripture to support any doctrine we embrace and any revelation we receive.

In today's church world there are those who have denied the inerrancy and absolute authority of the Scriptures and who are opening their minds to relative thinking and situation ethics. We cannot expect to receive revelation from God without accepting the fact that the Scriptures are not only inerrant truth but also our only source of absolute truth.

Throughout history men and women have written books containing their private revelations, attributing them to God while forming religious cults which have deceived many hearts and led many away from the truth. As Christians we must be careful never to open ourselves to what another claims to be "divine revelation" without scrutinizing his or her ideas against the written Word of God. *The Scriptures are the only basis for all true revelation.*

Evangelical Christians insist on two things about the Bible — that it is *divinely inspired* and that it has *absolute authority* in all matters of faith and practice. The Bible is not a record of man's quest for God as he has climbed the ladder of culture and civilization through the centuries. Rather, the Bible is an unfolding of God's truth to man so that man might find a path back to God and a basis for fellowship with Him.

Biblical Christianity is the revelation of God; it is not a man-made faith arrived at through the faulty guesses of men. The complete canon of Scripture — sixty-six books, no more, no less — is God's complete word to us. The Bible alone is the Word of God.

Divine Inspiration

It is altogether reasonable to believe that God chose to give man a trustworthy account of His revelation of truth. The record of this revelation — the Bible — is an infallibly inspired Book, given by God to man for his edification, guidance and blessing. This is a foundational belief of Christianity. Christianity stands or falls with the truth or falsehood of the Bible.

If the Bible is only the work of men, we can never lean on it for spiritual support. If it is no more than a human work, it must be a mere compilation of the ideas of man about ethics and morality, interwoven with a record of Jewish history. But the Bible is more than the work of man; it is the inspired work and Word of God.

Evangelical Christians in all parts of the world are united on the doctrine of the inspiration of the Holy Scriptures. However, there is an amazing divergence of opinion today about what is meant by *inspiration.* This divergence is problematic because if there is one truth in which Christians must be firmly established, it is the doctrine of the inspiration of the Holy Scriptures. We must be agreed not only about the fact of inspiration, but about the method of inspiration as well.

Inspiration Defined

Inspiration is a special act of the Holy Spirit by which He guided the writers of Scripture, making sure that their words were free from error and omission and that they conveyed the thoughts which the Holy Spirit desired. Our modern word *inspired* comes from the Latin and means "inbreathed." The Greek word *theopneustos* combines "God" and "breath." *Theos* means "God" and *pneuma* means "breath." These two words combine in the Bible to make *theopneustos,* which is translated "inspired by God."

By inspired we mean that the contents of the Bible were communicated to the writers by the Holy Spirit. That which is inspired is God's Word — written by human hands, molded in some degree by human thought and using human words. Under the influence of the Holy Spirit the writers were prevented from writing anything but what God intended. God so controlled the writer that the words written were exact and correct.

Inerrancy and Infallibility Defined

Inerrancy means "the state of being free from error." *Infallibility* means "incapability of error." The Word of God is infallible because God Himself is infallible. What the Bible says is to be received as the infallible Word of the infallible God. To believe in the inerrancy and infallibility of the Scriptures is to believe that they are of divine authorship and that God and His Word can be totally relied upon.

The infallibility of the Bible applies to the original manuscripts, not to translations and versions. However, competent scholars have brought our English versions to a remarkable degree of perfection, and we can with confidence rest in the belief that they are authoritative.

The evangelical Christian finds himself in violent disagreement with both the liberal and the neo-orthodox theologians. The liberal denies the infallible inspiration of the Word; the neo-orthodox believes that only those parts of the Bible which become significant to him as he reads them have authority. Some believe that the Bible is an imperfect instrument through which Christ, who is God's Word to man, is revealed. This implies that we cannot have confidence in the Bible.

What then is perfect, and what is imperfect? The answer comes through strong and clear in an anonymous quotation:

> Scripture is from God! Scripture is throughout from God; Scripture throughout is entirely from God. The Bible is God speaking in man; it is God speaking by man; it is God speaking as man! It is God speaking for man; but always it is God speaking.

Fallible Writers

God created man by breathing into him the breath of life so that man became a "living soul." In similar manner God breathed into the writers of Holy Scripture so that each could record the inspired Word of God. The Bible never states that the *men* who wrote were inspired; only their writings were inspired. The men were fallible; the Scripture they wrote is infallible.

Moses lost his temper and killed a man, but that does not change the fact that the Holy Spirit kept him from error as he wrote the Pentateuch. A similar statement could be made about David. He sinned, yet God used him to record portions of the infallible Word.

To accept the infallibility of the Scriptures written by fallible men, it may be helpful to draw an analogy between Jesus and the authorship of the Bible. In the conception of Jesus, the Holy Spirit came upon Mary and the "power of the Most High" overshadowed her so that the holy person born of her was called the Son of God (Luke 1:35).

Jesus was a Jew, not a Latin, a Nordic, an Indian or a Negro. He was recognizable as a man, and no doubt He had the physical characteristics of the Jewish race. Yet, He was also divine — the Son of God.

The Holy Spirit came upon the virgin Mary and caused her to conceive the human Jesus in her womb. In a similar manner the Holy Spirit overshadowed the mental faculties of the authors of Holy Writ and caused them to write the Bible. Their writings bear the stamp of human personality. The characteristics and vocabulary of the individuals are evident.

But the writings are not contaminated with human failure, despite personality characteristics, any more than the physical Jewish characteristics of Jesus lessened His absolute deity.

We know what God did even though we do not know how He did it. God gave us the Living Word free from sin and the written Word free from error.

Verbal Inspiration

Verbal inspiration means that every word in the original manuscripts was inspired by God. Yet we do not mean to say that the writers were mere secretaries who took dictation from the Almighty. The writers of Scripture were not robots. Each Bible writer used only those words in his vocabulary which the Holy Spirit approved and prompted him to use. In some cases this was direct dictation, such as when Moses wrote the exact directions God gave for the tabernacle. In other cases it was less direct, but no less exact.

God used forty men to write the sixty-six books. No two men were alike, but God used the vocabularies, styles and personalities of each writer to record His exact revelation. In other words, human authorship was respected to the extent that the characteristics of the writers were preserved and their styles and vocabularies were employed without error. This involved a mysterious interaction between the Spirit of God and man.

Plenary Inspiration

Plenary inspiration means full inspiration rather than partial inspiration of all Scripture. Verbal inspiration brings an accuracy that insures full inspiration for every portion of the Bible.

Thus the whole Bible is God's inspired, infallible Word written by fallible men. Different parts were produced under different kinds of inspiration:

1. There was divine guidance in the narration of facts and the selection of facts to be recorded in cases where the author related scenes and sayings which he had personally observed.

2. There was inspiration resulting from the operation of the Holy Spirit on the human faculties on those occasions when the writing was not a narration of past events, a prediction of future events or a declaration of the way of salvation. On the contrary, the writing was an expression of great moral and spiritual truth.

3. There was divine guidance when a writer brought forth God's thoughts on great doctrines and moral issues or when he expressed the inner thoughts of someone being written about. To illustrate — Matthew, when writing of the woman with the issue of blood, said, "For she said within herself" (Matt. 9:21). How could Matthew know what she said within herself unless the Holy Spirit had revealed it to him?

Inspiration Declared in Scripture

The historic doctrine of the verbal, plenary inspiration of the Bible is under grave attack today. However, the Christian must not base his defense of this vitally important doctrine upon the fact that it is historic. The doctrine must be defended because the Lord Jesus Christ and the Bible itself declare and demand it. Revelation of the Living Word to our hearts is impossible without it.

When asked by the Pharisees to solve a dispute, Jesus answered, "What is written in the law?" (Luke 10:26). The apostle Paul in a similar vein said, "What saith the scripture?" (Rom. 4:3; Gal. 4:30). Unquestionably the Scriptures teach their own inspiration. As we search the Scriptures we find the words "thus saith the Lord" or their equivalent almost two thousand times — thirteen hundred times in the prophetic books alone.

The testimony of Christ to the inspiration and authority of the Old Testament is beyond question. Not only did Christ meet each assault of Satan by quoting Scripture, but He also repeatedly referred to the occurrence of events in His life as the fulfillment of Scripture.

The apostle Paul verified the divine inspiration of Scripture when he stated that *all* Scripture is God-breathed (see 2 Tim. 3:16). He established the divine Source of the Old Testament by declaring that God "at sundry times and in divers manners spoke in time past unto the father by the prophets" (Heb. 1:1) and of the New Testament by claiming that the gospel he preached came to him by direct revelation from God (Gal. 1:12). Peter stated that no prophecy came by the will of man, but came from God as man was "moved by the Holy Ghost" (2 Pet. 1:21).

The Authority of the Scriptures

Which things also we speak, not in the words which man's wisdom teacheth, but which the Holy Ghost teacheth; comparing spiritual things with spiritual (1 Cor. 2:13).

For this cause also thank we God without ceasing, because, when ye received the word of God which ye heard of us, ye received it not as the word of men, but as it is in truth, the word of God, which effectually worketh also in you that believe (1 Thess. 2:13).

The Word of God is complete. It needs no additions and tolerates no subtractions (Rev. 22:18-19). The Bible has the authority to control our actions and give us answers to our questions. It is the infallible, authoritative rule of faith and conduct.

As God's authoritative Word, the Bible is the expression of God's will. Ignorance of the Bible inevitably produces ignorance of God's will for our lives. If the Bible is the authoritative expression of God's will for our lives, it must have priority in our interest and study. Our chief concern must be to understand this Book. Since knowledge of the Bible will bring us to decision, the Bible will be either a minister of life or of death to us. Our obedience will be the determining factor.

Apart from the conclusive proofs provided above, we have the witness of John Wesley. It was he who brought logic to bear on the infallibility and divine inspiration of the Word of God. He declared:

> I beg leave to give a short, clear, strong argument for the Divine inspiration of the Holy Scriptures. The Bible must be the invention of good men or angels, bad men or devils, or of God. It could not be the invention of good men or angels, for they neither would nor could make a book and tell lies all the time they were writing it, saying, "Thus saith the Lord," when it was their own invention. It could not be the invention of bad men or devils, for they could not make a book which commands all duty, forbids all sins, and condemns their own souls to Hell for all eternity. Therefore I draw the conclusion that the Bible must be given by Divine inspiration.[1]

As we determine that the written scriptures are our

only basis for divine revelation, we can safely move to the next step for receiving revelation: hearing. Our ability to hear the Word of God is affected by many external influences as well as some internal ones. How effectively we learn to hear the Word of God will be determined by the degree to which we appropriate to our own lives the principles of scripture about receiving divine revelation.

But blessed are your eyes, for they see: and your ears, for they hear. For verily I say unto you, that many prophets and righteous men have desired to see those things which ye see, and have not seen them; and to hear those things which ye hear, and have not heard them.

Matthew 13:16-17

4

How to Hear the Voice of God

Scriptural Principles for Hearing

Most of us have tried to communicate an important message to someone and felt that, though the person heard our words, he did not understand our message. Have you ever spoken earnestly to a friend and, by your friend's response, realized he had not really heard you? He listened to your words but did not hear your heart. Instead, he interpreted what you said according to his own preconceived attitude, perspective, prejudice or emotional response.

Just as radio signals are assigned to different wavelengths, so every person seems to have a certain wavelength by which he or she receives and interprets communicated information. That wavelength may be determined by many factors: background, culture, education, present desires and motivation, or past wounds and preconceived attitudes. There are many other influences as well that can affect a person's ability to hear accurately what a teacher, spouse or friend is saying to him. Daily stress, preoccupation with life, fatigue levels and other physical limitations may affect the way a person hears what is being said at a given moment.

We cannot escape these realities when we approach the Word of God to listen to what He is saying. How accurately we hear and interpret the scriptures depends on how well we have been able to receive information on "wavelengths" other than the one to which we are normally tuned in. To use biblical terms, we are all struggling with a natural man that chooses to live on the wavelength of independence from God and His Word. And we who are believers have a spiritual man that longs to hear the Word of God.

Our natural ears are conditioned, as has been mentioned, by many worldly influences that hinder the spiritual man from hearing the heart of God. Even when we read the Word, if we have not learned to yield to the Holy Spirit and to allow Him to teach us, we will not comprehend its true meaning. When Jesus quoted the prophet, Isaiah, saying that people have ears to hear yet they hear not (Matt. 13:14), He did not mean that the people He was referring to were physically deaf. He meant that though they were listening to words in their language, using their vocabulary, they had no understanding of the message He was trying to communicate. The words they heard either communicated something different to their minds than what He was actually saying or communicated nothing at all.

The Art of Listening

Apart from what I have just said, one of the main hindrances to hearing is that we are sorely lacking in the cultivation of the fine art of listening. How many times do exasperated parents say to their distracted child, "You are not listening to me." The child's mind is filled with his or her own pursuits of the moment, and has not been trained to listen to another's instruction. In universities and seminaries there are many classes offered on the art of communicating and speaking. I wonder how many classes are available to students to teach them the art of listening.

The inability to listen is one of the basic causes for relationship difficulties. Surely if it affects the natural realm of relationship so drastically, we must expect it to interfere dramatically with the spiritual realm as well. To begin with, we are far more familiar and comfortable with the natural realm than with the spiritual realm. We learned as infants to listen, and we have developed that natural trait largely through the natural world. When we are born again, we have to start from scratch to learn to listen with our spiritual ears to the truths of God.

Though the natural life and the spiritual life are two distinct realms, we cannot separate them totally in the living of our lives. Though God speaks to our spirits, we must comprehend what He has said with our minds and emotions and respond with our wills. Our souls must learn to recognize the voice of the Spirit. If we have not learned the natural art of listening, we must certainly expect to have greater difficulty hearing spiritual truths, no matter how clearly they are stated for us.

Everett L. Worthington, Jr., described the art of listening very clearly when he wrote:

> Attending is serious business. It is hard work. It is listening plus, which communicates active involvement. It is the cornerstone of a helping relationship. Listening involves more than hearing words. It involves eye contact, concern, discernment, paying attention to emotions, caring, feeling what the other person is feeling, watching for underlying motives and being aware of facial expressions. This involvement shows empathy, acceptance, and attentiveness on the part of the listener. Listening involves asking the right questions or making appropriate comments at the proper moment to encourage the person to go deeper into his or her feelings and concerns. Sometimes it is sitting in silence with someone without feeling the overwhelming need to say anything.[1]

Listening is the best remedy for loneliness, loquaciousness and laryngitis. Being a good listener is a wonderful gift, and yet few of us make much effort to cultivate it. We are a generation of communicators. We want our ideas to be heard, our positions to be understood, our emotions to be felt by our listeners. As a consequence, we have not given ourselves to the art of listening. Those of us who determine to do so will be amazed at what we actually *hear.*

Hearing Defined

There are several words used in the original languages of the scriptures that are translated into English as "listen" or "hear." Because we have only one word for "hear" we have not always understood clearly what God meant when He used the term. It will be insightful for us to explore briefly the related meanings of some of these original words translated as "listening" or "hearing."

When Jesus told the people that John the Baptist was "he, of whom it is written, Behold, I send my messenger before thy face, which shall prepare thy way before thee" (Matt. 11:10), He followed that revelation with the comment, "He who has ears to hear, let him hear" (v. 15). The Greek word for "hear" used by Jesus in the statement (*akouo*) means to hear in a natural sense with the ears and to understand the words that are spoken. Jesus used the same word when He spoke of what He had heard from the Father: "I have many things to say and to judge of you: but He that sent Me is true; and I speak to the world those things which I have heard of Him" (John 8:26). The intimate relationship the Father enjoyed with the Son, communing with Him while He was here on earth, is implied in this "hearing." How God wants His children to hear and understand His heart in the words He has given us!

A more powerful Greek word translated as "hear"

is *eisakouo,* which means "to hear and obey" and "to hear so as to answer." When the angel visited Zacharias in the temple, He said to him, "Fear not, Zacharias: for thy prayer is heard; and thy wife Elisabeth shall bear thee a son, and thou shalt call his name John" (Luke 1:13). In the sense in which the word is used in this scripture, to be heard by God is to be answered. What an amazing thought, that we could make a request of God and upon His hearing it, it is done! For our part, to hear the Word of God in this way means instant obedience to that Word.

When Felix responded to the charges against Paul, he said, "I will hear thee...when thine accusers are also come" (Acts 23:35). He used the Greek word for "hear" that means to hear fully and completely in a judicial sense. How important it is that we be willing to hear fully what God wants to say to us. To be a deliberate listener with the intention of judging God's Word to be true and then applying it should be the goal of every Christian.

The Greek word translated for "heard" (*epakroao-mai*) in the story about the prisoners who were listening to Paul and Silas praying and singing praises in their cell at midnight means "to listen attentively, with rapt attention." The prisoners were fascinated that these men, fellow prisoners, beaten and bleeding, were singing praises to their God at midnight. *How* we listen is as important as listening itself. If we are distracted by our own thoughts or interests, we cannot really hear what God is saying to us.

It is also possible to hear amiss or imperfectly or to hear without taking heed to what we have heard. When Jesus was giving us instructions about being reconciled to our brother, He said: "And if he shall neglect to hear (*parakouo*) them [the witnesses], tell it unto the church" (Matt. 18:17). It is always destructive in some way for us to choose not to hear the truth. We need to apply these and other biblical meanings of "hearing" to our lives in order to reap the benefits of truly hearing the voice of God.

As we cultivate the art of listening to other people and learn what it really means to hear, we will be better prepared to hear the voice of God. We must learn to practice the following scriptural principles in order to hear the voice of God. When we have mastered them, we will enjoy a relationship with God that we thought was either impossible or possible only for a select few.

Realize God Wants to Talk to Us

From my distress I called upon the Lord;
The Lord answered me and set me in a large
place (Ps. 118:5, NAS).

Perhaps as serious a hindrance to our ability to hear God's voice as not having the needed listening skills is not understanding that God desires to talk to us. He loves to answer our cry to Him. Because of our estrangement from the spiritual world in which God lives, we may find it incredible that an omnipotent, omniscient God would really want to communicate His heart to one such as ourselves. Even an intellectual acceptance of the fact that God's Word is His love story to us does not help us to grasp the reality that God Himself longs to communicate to each of us personally.

Yet the scriptures are full of examples of God's

answering those who called upon His name. God walked and talked with Abraham, telling him that Sarah would bear him a son within a year. God also warned Abraham that He was about to destroy Sodom and Gomorrah. Then God allowed Abraham to intercede with Him for the life of his nephew, Lot.

"Moses and Aaron were among His priests, And Samuel was among those who called on His name; They called upon the Lord, and He answered them. He spoke to them in the pillar of cloud" (Ps. 99:6-7, NAS). Scripture after scripture declares that God at times communicated directly with His people. Other verses indicate that He also spoke to them through His prophets to let them know His desires for them.

The reason God supernaturally gave us the written Word and has preserved it throughout the tragic history of mankind is so that He could reveal His heart to us through His words to us. We need to allow the wonderful reality of His love to settle into our hearts and help us realize that God does want us to hear Him. As we learn to cultivate the art of listening and believe that God wants to communicate to us personally, we will hear the voice of God and be transformed by what we hear Him say to us.

Cultivate Quietness

"Be still and know that I am God" (Ps. 46:10). The natural man in each of us is seldom prone to cultivate quietness. This is true to such an extent that quietness is sometimes linked with depression or sadness. We often ask someone who is not overly talkative, "Is something wrong?" Though withdrawal can sometimes relate to sadness, quietness itself should not be categorized as a sign of emotional distress.

It is not uncommon to see men and women walking or running in a beautiful park, plugged into their portable tape players and listening to their favorite music. The natural sounds of the birds and the water lapping against the shore go unnoticed. There seems to be an obsession in our culture to keep noise coming into our ears at all times. This must surely produce a dullness that will inoculate us against hearing what is important. It is almost as if there is a fear of silence in our culture today. What is the source of that fear? Are we afraid to be alone with our thoughts? Do we live in such inner unrest that we must escape the pain of it by continually putting external sounds into our natural ears?

One translation of the verse, "Be still, and know that I am God" declares, "Cease striving and know that I am God" (Ps. 46:10, NAS). There is more to quietness than an absence of external noise. There is a cessation of our frantic thoughts and pursuits, our insatiable desires and selfish motivations. As we cultivate that kind of quietness, we are promised that we will know God. His thoughts toward us will become a reality in our lives, and personal revelation of His love will fill our hearts. That in turn will cause us to cease the more from striving because of the satisfaction to our souls that we enjoy with Him.

When the prophet Elijah was in deep distress, running for his life from the wicked Jezebel, he had some dramatic experiences with the Lord. The Lord came to him and asked him what he was doing in a cave, running for his life. After Elijah answered Him, the Lord commanded him to stand on the mountain, and a strong wind that broke rocks passed by. But the Lord was not in the wind. And after the wind an earthquake occurred, but the Lord was not in the earthquake. And after the earthquake, Elijah saw a fire, but the Lord was not in the fire. And after all these things, there was a sound of gentle blowing out of which the Lord spoke and gave Elijah the direction he needed (1 Kin. 19:9-18, NAS). Though God's voice was sometimes heard in the scriptures as thunder from heaven, He chose to speak to Elijah in what we have called "the still small voice."

If we fail to cultivate quietness before God, we will surely miss hearing His voice. If we come to Him and say everything that is on our hearts, but fail to wait for Him to speak to us, we cannot expect to hear Him. How ludicrous it would be for me to be traveling and decide to call my husband, Leroy, at home yet not let him talk to me. We would consider it foolish if I picked up the telephone, dialed home, greeted Leroy and told him about my trip and then abruptly said, "Well, good-bye, Honey, I love you." The reason I called was to hear his voice and find out how he is. I want him to return my expression of love and respond to what I am saying.

Yet how many of us use our time of prayer to make all our requests and then say, "I love you, Lord, see you later," without waiting for a response from Him? We have been schooled by our religious tradition to believe that talking with God is a one-way proposition. It is not. If we will dare to quiet ourselves to listen to God, we will hear His loving voice.

Meditating on the Word

> Blessed is the man that walketh not in the
> counsel of the ungodly, nor standeth in the
> way of sinners, nor sitteth in the seat of the
> scornful. But his delight is in the law of the
> Lord; and in his law doth he meditate day
> and night (Ps. 1:1-2).

The scriptures clearly endorse the value and necessity of meditating on the Word of God. Joshua, as the new leader of Israel who was to take the people into the Promised Land, was commanded: "This book of the law shall not depart out of thy mouth; but thou shalt meditate therein day and night that thou mayest observe to do according to all that is written therein: for then thou shalt make thy way prosperous, and then thou shalt have good success" (Josh. 1:8). His success was dependent upon his meditating on the law continually so that he would know and observe it.

The Hebrew word *hagah* that is translated "meditate" in this passage is the same word that the psalmist used to describe the blessed man who delights in the law of the Lord. It means "to ponder, to murmur or mutter and study." It implies a careful reading and serious attitude that will allow the reader to understand the Word in such a way that he or she will obey it. We are instructed to meditate on the Word continually, day and night. What transformation would occur in the thought life of most Christians if we would obey this scriptural command.

Meditating on the scriptures will help us to understand the way God thinks, His principles and His attitude toward sin as well as His love for the sinner. We will become familiar with God's vocabulary, and learn what He expects us to do in order to please Him. As we fill our minds with God's words, we will be able to discern the difference between His voice and the voice of our accuser, the devil. And we will be able to know the difference as well between the condemning voices of our own flesh or that of other people and the loving acceptance of our God.

Unfortunately, because of our frantic, noise-filled lifestyles, meditation for most of us is a lost art. For many, our only reference to meditation is as a part of the eastern religions and cults that, while cultivating the art of meditation, have lost the God who commanded it. Until we decide to cultivate the quietness of waiting on God and meditating on His Word, we cannot expect to hear His voice.

Ask God Questions

> Then the Lord answered Job out of the whirlwind (Job 38:1).

If Judson Cornwall were visiting me in my home as I was reading one of his books, I would not ask someone else what he meant if I had a question about what I was reading. I would ask him. As logical as that may seem, we often ask other people our questions regarding the scriptures we have read, rather than asking the Author Himself.

Many times as I have meditated on the Word and asked God about something I did not understand, He would begin to give me understanding through another verse that shed light on the one I was questioning or otherwise open my understanding to the truth He was revealing. Sometimes one tiny verse would take me through the scriptures, opening a concept or truth that I had not understood. It is the Holy Spirit's task to lead us into all truth (John 16:13). God knew we needed an instructor. That is why He sent the Holy Spirit to be our divine Teacher. He welcomes our questions and is there to answer them for us.

Anticipate Hearing God Speak

> Unto thee will I cry, O Lord my rock; be not
> silent to me (Ps. 28:1).

From the creation of mankind in the garden of Eden, God has desired to commune with His people. It is the Spirit-filled believer who has the greatest potential for hearing God's voice, because God dwells in our hearts by His Holy Spirit. We are His temples. As we quiet our minds and open our hearts to His Word, we can anticipate hearing the voice of God communing with us, Spirit to spirit.

There is nothing in all the earth that thrills me more than to have my Lord talk to me. It causes my spirit to leap within me like the babe did in the womb of Elizabeth. I am changed and strengthened and convinced of His love for me as He speaks even a single word. His correction is as welcome as His commendation — just so I can hear His voice. That hearing is a result of the relationship that we cultivate with God by following the commands of scripture to quiet ourselves in His presence and meditate on His Word.

Respond to What You Hear

> But prove yourselves doers of the word, and
> not merely hearers who delude themselves
> (James 1:22, NAS).

After we have heard God, it is imperative that we obey what He has said. The scriptures are meant to be obeyed, not just meditated upon. The apostle James warned us of the deception that comes when we are hearers of the Word only and not doers of it. Perhaps this is one of the greatest reasons Christians complain that they no longer hear God speak to them: They have not obeyed the last thing He said for them to do.

The scriptures teach that obedience is better than sacrifice (Ps. 51:16). How many times have we found it easier to enter into a "sacrifice" rather than to obey the simple command that has been given us? Working for God is wonderful when it is out of obedience to God's will for our lives. But we dare not think that our sacrifice for Him is of any value if we are not continually being guided by His voice and fulfilling His commands. Doing good things is not the same as being obedient to the voice of God. That is why it is imperative that we learn to hear His voice.

Look for Confirmation

> Every fact is to be confirmed by the testimo-
> ny of two or three witnesses (2 Cor. 13:1).

If we feel we have gained an insight into the scriptures, we need to be willing to let it be judged by other scriptures as well as by other men and women of God who know how to hear His voice. Too many times believers have twisted the meaning of a verse of Scripture to meet their own desires or bring judgment on another's situation. It is important that we look for confirmation of every revelation that we receive.

Even sincere believers have erred in their interpretation of the scriptures and have preached the error as truth, bringing harm to the body of Christ. We need to be sensitive and discerning to the voice of God as well as submissive to other men and women of God who can confirm or correct our "revelations." A true understanding of the scriptures will always bear the nature of Christ and never violate any other principle in the Bible.

Personal guidance and prophetic words we receive from the Holy Spirit should be confirmed by the written Word, by the peace they bring to our spirits and by mature members of the body of Christ before we decide to obey them. We are too vulnerable to the other voices of the flesh, the enemy and other people not to seek confirmation of every directive that comes to us. There is safety in a multitude of counsel.

Remember His Words

> But the lovingkindness of the Lord is from everlasting to everlasting...to those who keep His covenant, And who remember His precepts to do them (Ps. 103:17-18).

To say that we need to remember the words God speaks to us may seem too obvious. But how many of us have received prophetic words and have transcribed them and filed them away, without remembering what God had promised to do when He spoke those words to us? An entire book of the Bible, Deuteronomy, was written to help the children of Israel remember what God had done and what He had commanded them to do. It is important to remember the words of God to us.

The enemy tries to defeat us by causing us to forget that God loves us, as He tells us so clearly in His Word. Our minds need to not only meditate continually on the Word of God, but also remember the wonderful ways God has changed us and revealed Himself to us through His Word.

If we will follow these principles for hearing the voice of God, our lives will be transformed by His presence in our lives. Then we can begin to unlock the beautiful truths in the scriptures as we give ourselves to the study of the language or vocabulary of God. Every word of God is like a multifaceted diamond which when held up to the light of the Holy Spirit, glistens with revelatory truth for the one who will pursue the eternal truths they communicate.

———— ❀ ————

And...having made peace
through the blood of His
cross; through Him [Christ],
I say, whether [they be] things
on earth or things in
heaven...He has now
reconciled you in His fleshly
body through death, in order
to present you before Him
holy and blameless and
beyond reproach.

Colossians 1:20, 22, NAS

5

The Language of Scripture

Establishing the Validity of Revelation

It is vital that we be able to interpret rightly the language of Scripture if we are to walk in divine revelation. An intellectual approach to understanding the Scriptures will not result in correct interpretation of the truth they contain.

The Scriptures are clear regarding the state of our carnal mind, declaring it to be hostile to God and unable to submit to the law of God (Rom. 8:7). The Scriptures also declare that the natural man cannot receive the things of God, because they are foolishness to him (1 Cor 2:14). Unfortunately, many educated men and women who have studied the Scriptures have interpreted them according to the understanding of the unredeemed intellect, instead of relying on the Holy Spirit to reveal to them the precious truths of God's Word.

As we consider the fact that all language is under the curse of sin, we realize that we cannot possibly understand the true meaning of God's written message to us without the work of the Holy Spirit to reveal to us its intent.

After the fall of man, while there was still only one language on earth, human communication developed without the knowledge of God. That led to the pride, rebellion and sin which inspired the building of the tower of Babel. When God saw that men were trying to reach Him by their own efforts, He came and confused their tongues. The many languages which resulted kept them from uniting in rebellion.

It is interesting to note that man's language was confused by God as a result of pride. For this reason, the opposite of pride, humility, is required for us to speak in an unknown tongue and receive the baptism of the Holy Spirit. Speaking in tongues is foolishness to our minds. But it is a verbal expression that our three enemies — the world, the flesh and the devil — cannot interpret and that edifies our spirits.

It is the enemy's work to confuse our study of the Scriptures by perverting the vocabulary through which God intended to communicate spiritual truths to us. Our understanding of language must be redeemed to allow us to interpret properly the divine message of the Scriptures. If we are not aware of the battle for our minds between the two kingdoms of light and darkness, we will not understand the confusion of terms.

Two Kingdoms

GOD'S WORD

heaven... light... love...
faith in God...

EARTH AND DARKNESS

Satan's perversions: false gods...
lust... materialism...

In the diagram above, the top half-circle represents light and life. The bottom half-circle represents darkness and death. The cross connecting the two halves represents the sacrifice of Christ that made it possible for us to be delivered from darkness and reconciled to the light of God.

Satan lived in the realm of light before he became

Satan. He was Lucifer, the highest of all archangels. He was a chorister — the music director, the worship leader of the angels. In a supernatural way that we cannot comprehend, music actually flowed through him in creativity (Ezek. 28:13-14). But Lucifer rebelled and was kicked out of heaven along with a third of the angels.

Heavenly Vocabulary Perverted

While Lucifer was in heaven, he learned God's vocabulary. When he became the prince and power of the air, he brought the language of heaven to earth. But he twisted it and used heavenly words to mean something that are at best perversions of their true meaning.

For example, to people under the power of Satan in the kingdom of darkness the word *love* means any lewd, perverted emotional attachment or feeling they want it to mean. That definition bears little resemblance to the beauty of the character of God, who is Love. The word's original intent was to describe God. We can experience affection, infatuation and admiration without knowing the love of God. But pure love *is* God. And the more we have of God, the more capacity we have for love.

The Scriptures teach that Satan is a thief and the father of lies. He cannot create anything, so he tries to duplicate the qualities of the kingdom of light and pervert their meaning in the kingdom of darkness. For example, Satan has perverted the use of the word *faith* to justify a belief in anything — it doesn't matter if you are a Buddhist or a humanist as long as you have "faith" in something. He has done that in an attempt to destroy the uniqueness of our faith in God. God never intended for our faith to be placed in false gods or self-realization.

The idea of *wisdom* in the kingdom of light and in the kingdom of darkness are also two different things. Without God *wisdom* refers to earthly knowledge — mere intellect — which can never comprehend the kingdom of light. Godly wisdom belongs to another world, and only One Person, the Holy Spirit who came from heaven to help us, can open the Scriptures and reveal godly wisdom to us.

The Holy Spirit wrote the Book and then moved into our temples to teach it to us. He came as the Teacher to take up His residence in our spirits and to tell us what He meant when He wrote it. He gives revelation of the wisdom we are seeking. This Wisdom is Jesus, the King of the kingdom of light, who was made unto us wisdom (1 Cor. 1:30).

Language of Types and Shadows

When our infinite God desired to communicate with finite men, He had to find ways for us to understand what He was saying. Because of sin, men's minds could not comprehend a God who was holy and absolute. So God reached into our world and used human language to reveal His will for mankind. He spoke to men through parables, metaphors, similes, hyperboles, types and allegories. Using these linguistic tools, God unfolded in His Word beautiful truths about Himself and His purposes for mankind.

A careful foundation must be laid for the understanding of type and allegory so that we do not violate the true meaning of the Scriptures. A *type* is a person, thing or event which represents another, especially another that is to come in the future. Typology, the study of types, can bring to light many precious truths in the Word of God which are otherwise hidden to us. We can discover these truths as silver is discovered — by descending into a dark mine shaft and digging for them.

An *allegory* is a story in which people, things and happenings have a symbolic significance — not merely a literal one — which is often morally instructive. For example, when Jesus taught about the shepherd who searched for his lost sheep, He was not telling the story of a specific event that happened in Galilee. He was using this allegorical picture of a shepherd's care for his sheep to show the Father's love and care for each of His children.

David portrayed the Lord allegorically as a Shepherd in the poetic psalm that has spoken comfort to us throughout the centuries — Psalm 23. How beautifully his word pictures help to reveal the nature of God to us!

To properly understand type and allegory, we must realize that it is not possible to make every word in a story fit a divine truth. Usually one or two spiritual truths can be uncovered from the description of an otherwise natural event. We must be careful not to try to find types in every intricate detail of an allegory that was written to reveal only a few major truths. No earthly story completely symbolizes an eternal truth.

For example, Abraham represents God the Father in Scripture. Yet we see that Abraham sometimes did not act like God. Because of his humanity he could not be a perfect type of the heavenly Father. In the same way Joseph is perhaps the most complete type of Christ in the Bible. Over three hundred comparisons can be made between his life and the life of Christ. But he was not a perfect man. These men did live out certain truths in their natural lives, however, that help us receive a spiritual message from a spiritual country and King.

We must make sure that the truth revealed in a type or allegory can go through the cross. That is to say, the truth it teaches must relate without question to God's eternal plan for the salvation of mankind that was fulfilled through the shedding of Jesus' blood on Calvary.

Each truth that is concealed in a type in the Old Testament is revealed in the New Testament reality of Jesus' sacrifice for the sin of mankind. Types and allegories are valid revelation only as they help us apply truth to our lives and as they agree with all other Scripture.

The ultimate purpose for all revelation must be to transform us into the image of Christ.[1] The study of types and shadows and other "picture" language that God used to communicate divine truths to us will unlock His great heart of love for us.

Names and Places

Our study of the Scriptures will be greatly enriched by considering the meanings of names and places. As we properly identify the people recorded in the Scriptures and begin to understand their background and culture, we will receive light on the truths they represent.

In ancient cultures, titles and names carried much greater significance than they do in most of our modern cultures. Old Testament names often revealed one's character prophetically. For example, Jacob's name means "supplanter and cheater." Those qualities characterized his life as he sought to take the blessing of God from his brother, Esau.

In some instances, names were given to mark an event in history. When the glory of God departed from the house of Israel while the wife of the priest was giving birth, she named her son Ichabod, which means "the glory is departed" (1 Sam. 4:21).

Names were changed for specific reasons, often to mark an encounter with God. When God established the covenant with Abram, He changed Abram's name to Abraham, adding the *h* with the rough breathing sound "ha" that represents the breath of God. Thus the name *Abraham* refers to the experience this man's encounter with the living God, one that transformed his life forever.

In the New Testament, Jesus called Simon to be His disciple. Simon means "reed" and carries the connotation of weakness and instability. Jesus changed Simon's name to Peter, which means "rock," signifying prophetically the strength of character this apostle would one day demonstrate in the kingdom of God.

Many other examples could be given of Bible characters whose names were changed as a result of the redeeming power of God which touched their lives. Understanding their significance is important to receiving the revelation they bring.

There are entire books of the Bible whose truths are unlocked to us through an understanding of the names of its characters. The book of Ruth is one example of such a book. The setting for the book is the town of Bethlehem-judah. *Bethlehem* means "house of bread." *Judah* signifies "a place where people praise God." The name *Bethlehem-judah* characterizes life as a place of bountiful provision and joy.

As the book opens we are introduced to the family of Elimelech who are living in the land of Bethlehem-judah. *Elimelech* means "God is King." Elimelech represents a godly man, rearing his children in a place of provision and praise. His wife's name is *Naomi,* which means "pleasant." Her presence in the home filled it with pleasantness for her husband and two sons as she nurtured her family in the place of praise. Their two sons were named *Mahlon* and *Chilion,* which mean "joy" and "song," respectively.

Allegorically, this family represents the redeemed church today whose lives are to be characterized as houses of bread and places of praise. Cultivating His presence in our lives as our King, we experience the pleasantness of His kingdom and are filled with joy and praise when we come to God's house to worship together.[2]

Then a famine came to the land, and Naomi's family left. Understanding the reasons for the famine in the land of Bethlehem-judah gives us further prophetic insight into the ways of God with His church.

Though Naomi's life was filled with so much such bitterness after leaving the house of bread that she wanted her name to be changed to *Mara* meaning "bitter," God in His mercy brought her back to the place of praise and brought wonderful redemption to her.

Reading the book of Ruth simply as an historical narrative would cause us to miss the revelatory prophetic truths it contains regarding the liberation of the believer from the land of famine and destitution and the wonderful relationship of the bride to her Bridegroom.

The kinsman-redeemer in the book of Ruth is Boaz, whose name means "redeemer." He is a beautiful type of Christ who is willing to love the "foreigner" and make her a part of his lineage. A simple study of the names and places in this book reveals the heart of the Father for the church as He reveals the plan of redemption and His desire to find a bride for His Son.

Searching out the types and shadows and the meanings of names and places will reward us with the riches of the wisdom that lie beneath the narrative. Even single-word studies on words such as *wisdom* or *love* will bring revelation to our minds of the true meaning of the language of God.

As we renew our minds with the beautiful language of the Scriptures, learning to think in terms that God intended, we will defeat the enemy's purpose in perverting God's vocabulary. We will also be laying a foundation to receive divine revelation from the Word of God. We must be careful to approach our study of the Word in the correct attitude in order to interpret properly its meaning. It could be accurately declared that our attitude determines our altitude.

Attitudes for Receiving Revelation

Anger and other negative emotions will influence our thinking and interpretation of the Scriptures if we try to, for example, "get back" at our enemies. When we are angry it is easy to quote David's "God get 'em" prayers over our enemies. However, Christ teaches us under the New Covenant that we must pray for our enemies. Even a know-it-all attitude can be detrimental to the study of the Word, since it can prevent us from being teachable and open to another's view.

One important attitude we must cultivate as we approach the Scriptures is *meekness*. The Scriptures themselves exhort us to "receive with meekness the engrafted word, which is able to save your souls" (James 1:21).

Humility is a synonym for the word *meekness* in this passage. Children expect to be taught and are usually eager to learn. They understand that they do not know what they need to know in any given situation, and they are willing to receive instruction. It is this attitude of humility with which we must approach the Scriptures, no matter how long we have been studying them, if we expect to have our ears open to receive new truth.

We also need to cultivate the attitude of a *servant* who expects to *do* the commands of his master, not just *hear* them. The apostle James admonishes us to be "doers of the Word and not hearers only, deceiving your own selves" (James 1:22).

God commanded Joshua to meditate day and night on the book of the Law and to keep all its commandments in order to have success in all he did (Josh. 1:8). Ultimately our obedience to the Word of God will determine the degree of success we enjoy in our relationship with God.

Determination to keep the Word of God and make it preeminent in our lives must characterize our study of the Scriptures. The church at Philadelphia was commended by the words, "and hast kept my word, and hast not denied my name" (Rev. 3:8).

Our own desires and the demands and philosophies of the world will continually threaten to erode our determination to walk in purity and integrity and obedience to the Scriptures. But the promise of the Scriptures is that the Word "is able to save your souls" (James 1:21). We must never allow our own thinking or another's opinion to deter us from tenaciously clinging to the Word of God as the source of our life and our salvation.

We must also be willing to "selah" the Word of God — that is, to take time to muse and meditate on it. The picture here is of a cow that chews its cud, eating first and then calmly regurgitating what it has eaten in order to chew it slowly until it is completely digested. The old adage to "take time to be holy" is not an option but a necessity if we are to commune with God and receive revelation from the Word that will change our lives.

Knowing the attitudes with which we should approach our study of the Word, we can appreciate more fully the wonderful process the Word of God works in us that brings us into revelation — revelation of not only the written Word, but also of the Living Word.

But we all, with open face beholding as in a glass the glory of the Lord, are changed into the same image from glory to glory, even as by the Spirit of the Lord.

2 Corinthians 3:18

6

The Process of Revelation

Seven Steps God's Word Works in Us

Revelation, the true unveiling of the life of Christ, becomes a reality in our lives as we allow the Holy Spirit to use the Word of God as a divine knife to split open the veil of flesh between our souls and spirits. The life of Christ that lives within us through the new birth or salvation experience is then unveiled to influence and transform our souls more and more into the image of God as we fill our inner man with the Word. As we yield to this divine process, the Holy Spirit reveals the Word in us and the life of Christ is expressed through our lives.

The apostle Paul declared that the divine life in us is "Christ in you, the hope of glory" (Col. 1:27). It is the wonderful Person of Jesus manifesting His life in our minds, wills and emotions that saves us from sin and self and shows the love of God to the world.

Many Christians are treating Jesus as the Israelites did. They were content for God to dwell in a box and have the priest go into His presence once a year. But that is not God's intent. As we have seen, God wants to walk with men and pour His life into them, communing with them Spirit to spirit.

Since the fall of man, He has been initiating tabernacles and temples through which He could reach man and fellowship with Him. In the wonderful redemption wrought through Christ, He has made it possible for each believer to become His temple. He intends for His temples to be filled with His glory, the Living Word, Christ Himself.

The prophet Isaiah saw the Lord "high and lifted up and His train *filled* the temple" (Is. 6:1). He witnessed the fullness of the glory of God. It is this fullness that we are beginning to experience in the church today. The best days for the church lie ahead of us. As we seek to know God through revelation, allowing Him to fill our individual temples, we will discover the Wisdom that created the universe.

The book of Proverbs teaches us how to find this Wisdom. The writer declares, "If thou seekest her as silver, and searchest for her as for hid treasures; Then shalt thou understand the fear of the Lord, and find the knowledge of God" (Prov. 2:4-5). Silver is not found lying on top of the ground; it must be mined.

In the Scriptures silver represents redemption. As we dig for silver in the Word of God, we will find Christ, who has been made unto us wisdom (1 Cor. 1:30).

We have stated that the Holy Spirit has come to split open the veil of flesh that covers our minds and to show us the things that are of Jesus (John 16:15). I wish I could say that the Holy Spirit does this instantaneously when we are born again, because that would fit our American mentality of "fast food" and "fast experience." However, that has not been my experience, nor do the Scriptures teach such immediate transformation. The apostle Paul understood the gradual nature of the process when he wrote:

> But we all, with open face beholding as in a glass the glory of the Lord, are changed into the same image from glory to glory, even as by the Spirit of the Lord (2 Cor. 3:18).

I have felt the Holy Spirit tearing my flesh, shining His light on a wrong attitude or concept. While still in pain, I have seen new dimensions of revelatory truth run from the Word through my spirit into my mind. As we continually allow this divine process in our lives, we discover that the life of Christ truly becomes our life.

His mind becomes our mind. We think differently about certain situations. Our carnal thoughts give way to the life-giving thoughts and perspective of Christ. We are renewed in the spirit of our mind as Paul exhorted us to be (Eph. 4:23).

The old man, our self life, is pressed out, and Christ possesses that inner part of us He bought for Himself for eternity. Only through the work of divine revelation is it possible for Him to possess the whole "temple."

When we are born again and Christ moves into the "holy of holies" of our temples, our spirits are recreated and we become alive to God. Once He resides in our temples, He has to function from the inside out in order for His life to reach our minds, our wills and our emotions. That is when He calls for the help of the Holy Spirit to open the way by dividing asunder the soul and the spirit, discerning the thoughts and intents of the heart (Heb. 4:12). In this way the Word of God becomes our life.

It is imperative that we fill our minds with the Word of God if we expect to receive divine revelation. That is how the Holy Spirit is able to show us the things of Jesus and shine His light on our carnality. As we obey Him and submit to the Word of God, revelation will come.

Jesus said it was expedient for Him to go away so that He could send us the Comforter who would give us the things of Jesus. The Holy Spirit comes in with a broom, a mop and soap, and as a refiner's fire He cleans up the mess in our souls — our wrong thinking, wrong choices and wrong emotional responses. We gave Him full permission to do this work when we invited the Holy Spirit to live in us.

Won't it be wonderful when the charismatic church begins to understand why the Holy Spirit came? He didn't come to give gifts; He brought spiritual gifts with Him as part of the package. He didn't come simply to cause us to speak in tongues. He came to unveil Christ in us and through us to the world. It is His work in us that will bring the answer to Christ's prayer "that they also may be one in us: that the world may believe that thou hast sent me" (John 17:21).

Divine revelation is not an exciting little idea that brings understanding about one scripture. It is the work of the Holy Spirit done inside of us as He unveils the Christ who is in us. The more He unveils His wisdom, the more that wisdom becomes our life, and the more Christlike we become.

We don't live the Christ life by trying to become like Christ — we cannot change ourselves. I tried for seventeen years as a dedicated Methodist professor — it didn't work. We must allow the Holy Spirit to come in and do for us what we cannot do for ourselves.

As the Holy Spirit works in us, He speaks the Word of God to us in such a way that it destroys the power of darkness and sin that has lived in our souls, and it brings the light of God to dispel our darkness. He can only do this wonderful, redemptive work, however, while we are cooperating with Him in reading the Word and meditating on its truths.

As we focus on the world of light presented in the Scriptures, the contrast to the world of darkness in our own souls and around us will become greater. There are seven steps the Word of God takes in us to dispel the darkness in us and transform us into the character of Christ.

The Process of Revelation

We have stated emphatically that there is no true revelation of God apart from the Word of God. The Holy Spirit has been given the task of unveiling Christ — the Living Word — in us through the application of the truth of the written Word to our lives. The written Word works in us a divine process of revelation that changes our lives.

1. Information

The first step toward revelation in this divine process is to receive *information*. We must first receive a basic truth in our minds and hearts in order for the Holy Spirit to bring it to our remembrance. We cannot expect this first step toward revelation to happen apart from spending time daily reading and meditating on the Word of God.

When our nation was first founded the Bible was the textbook used in our schools. Our children were taught the Scriptures as soon as they learned to read. They learned the Ten Commandments and studied the Old Testament patriarchs as well as the parables of Jesus. What a wonderful foundation those generations were given of the principles of God.

Today our children's minds are filled with worldly information, and many have never heard of the Old Testament patriarchs. They have not been given the opportunity to receive the information — the basic truth — of the Scriptures.

As Christians we need to spend time reading and memorizing the Word of God and teach our children to do likewise. This is the first step in making it possible for the Holy Spirit to do His wonderful work of bringing us divine revelation.

Joshua received a mandate that would guarantee his success — to meditate day and night on the law of God (Josh. 1:8). How faithfully we follow this same mandate will determine our success or failure in walking toward true revelation. Without a knowledge of the information contained in the Scriptures, we cannot have a fuller revelation of Christ within us, even if we are born-again Christians.

2. Illumination

Have you enjoyed the experience of reading a familiar passage of Scripture and suddenly having a light come on in your mind? You see how a principle applies to an area of your life, or perhaps you see why God responded to a person's plight in Scripture the way He did. In that moment, information has taken on another dimension — illumination.

When information begins to be a light to our spirits, it becomes *illumination*. We understand, in a way we never understood before, the truth we are reading that was once only information to us. At that point, it becomes our responsibility to walk in obedience to that truth.

3. Inspiration

As the Holy Spirit continues His process of bringing revelation to us, we find ourselves responding to the truth with His joy. The Holy Spirit receives the Word with joy, and as we receive it from Him, it becomes *inspiration* to us. New desires to obey the Word fill our hearts.

Inspiration makes us hungry for the Word of God. The divine work of the Holy Ghost makes us "hunger and thirst after righteousness" (Matt. 5:6). No person can make us hungry for the Word. If we find ourselves hungering for truth, we are receiving a new invitation from the Holy Spirit to receive greater revelation.

People who sit in church and are bored to death

with the preached Word are not hungry. We will eat anything when we are hungry. The Scriptures declare that to the hungry soul every bitter thing is sweet, but the full man loathes a honeycomb (Prov. 27:7). When we are hungry for the Word, we are saying we want more of God. The blessed Holy Spirit then splits the veil of our darkened minds and emotions and wills, and that part of Jesus which enters our ears becomes life on the inside.

4. New Revelation

The written Word of God (*logos*) can be viewed as a transcription of God's voice. When the transcribed Word moves from our heads to our hearts, inspiring us to its reality, it becomes a living Word to us (*rhema*). That living Word is *revelation*.

Revelation makes the truth become a living Person to us. As we respond to the revelation of that divine Person, we yield our wills, minds and emotions to His divine character of holiness and righteousness, and the life of Christ is unveiled within us. When the Holy Spirit breathes a revealed truth into our spirits, it becomes our life. We actually experience what we had previously heard only as information.

It is our obedience to the revelation we receive that enables the Holy Spirit to keep giving us new revelation. *Once revelation begins to flow in us, it keeps flowing unless we resist it.* It is a serious matter indeed to disobey divine revelation that has come to our hearts. Darkness is dispelled only by the light that pierces it. If we give place to darkness rather than walking in the light we have received, we will suffer the consequences of our disobedience.

5. Realization

After revelation begins to work in our hearts, the next step in the divine growth process is *realization*. Realization is the recognition that we are being changed through our obedience to the revelation that has become a part of our lives. We realize that the change that is taking place in us is reality. It affects the way we live.

We don't know exactly what happened, but we realize we are not losing our tempers like we used to. We realize we are walking in a grace we did not have before. Other people can observe this change in us. Our spirits are sensitive to the truth that has become a living reality in us, and we are careful not to disobey it.

6. Transformation

Transformation of our character occurs as we allow death to come to the self-life through the rending of the veil of flesh. Those deep, inward tendencies to self-centeredness and lack of love that reside in our natural man are fundamentally changed — transformed — into holy desires and the love of Christ for others. The life of Christ can then be lived through us in the world.

A consistent walk in greater depths of revelation brings a gradual *transformation* to our lives. We are changed from glory to glory into the image of the Son through our obedience to the revelation we receive.

7. Manifestation

The final step the Spirit of Truth works in us is the *manifestation* of Jesus' character in our lives. Maturity is the beauty of Jesus as it is seen in people who have allowed revelation to touch their lives in every area of their souls and spirits. In obedience to God they have continually turned from sin and allowed the nature of Christ to be fully unveiled in them.

The beautiful part of the process of revelation is that different truth may be at different stages in us at the same time. One truth may be at the fourth stage — that of revelation — becoming a reality to us and preparing us to move on to realization and transformation. Another truth we have just received as information may inspire us to seek God for revelation. In this way, as we consistently avail ourselves of the reading and hearing of the Word, the Holy Spirit takes the Book and writes it on our hearts.

Information is transferring my notes to your mind. It has no eternal value unless it goes beyond that. But in our search for wisdom, we pray that God will make His Word real to us and open our minds to receive divine revelation. It was the Son of God Himself who declared in the face of the tempter, "Man shall not live by bread alone, but by every word that proceedeth out of the mouth of God" (Matt. 4:4). It is God's proceeding Word that contains the power to save our souls (James 1:21).

Faith Comes by Hearing

The Scriptures teach that without faith it is impossible to please God (Heb. 11:6). They declare that faith comes by hearing and hearing by the Word of God (Rom. 10:17). The entrance of the living Word into our spirits is the natural ear. I often instruct people to read the Word aloud so their minds can't wander and so ears can hear it. Though it is not always appropriate to read the Word aloud, much good can come from reading this way.

We each have five sense gates in our bodies, and one of them is the hearing gate — our ears. Our sense of hearing is often the last faculty we lose before we leave this world.

There is no such thing as a person's being totally unconscious. Though medical science uses the term *unconscious* to indicate that the conscious mind is not responding to external stimuli, doctors understand that the unconscious person often hears everything around him. Sometimes people who come out of a coma repeat what was said about them around the bed.

I believe that God in His great mercy leaves the ear gate open to those who find themselves at death's door and have not accepted Christ as their Savior. God does not want anyone to go to hell. They can still hear the gospel and respond in faith in their hearts to one who prays with them.

It is a wise person who spends time daily reading and meditating on the Word of God, using helpful tools to study truths that are illumined to his or her heart. It is wisdom to sit under sound teaching of the Word, listening to those who are walking in revelation and preaching prophetically to the body of Christ.

In this way, we consistently fill our thoughts with life-giving words that displace our carnal reasoning and unbelief. We make it possible for the Holy Spirit to do His wonderful redemptive work of unveiling Christ to us continually.

How Revelation Deepens

We cannot underestimate the time and energy that is required to make us students of the Word who can receive an ever-greater revelation of God to our souls. We dare not expect to enter into intimate relationship with the almighty God as easily as we would microwave a potato or flip a light switch. Even human relationships require time to cultivate and nurture to any level of intimacy, whether in marriage or friendship.

It is as we give priority to the Word and learn to yield to the Holy Spirit when He speaks something fresh to us that we can be assured of deepening our relationship with God through revelation. It is a joy to me, after studying the Word since my youth, to have the Holy Spirit speak to me about a particular truth and then bring other scriptures to mind that shed light on it.

One "special session" I had with the Holy Spirit was quite unexpected and, at first, seemed untimely to me. I had had a hectic weekend. I ministered three times in Nashville, Tennessee, on Friday evening and Saturday. My traveling companion and I drove from there to Snellville, Georgia, arriving about 10:30 P.M. on Saturday evening. I preached Sunday morning, afternoon and evening there. Then we got up at 5:00 A.M. to travel home for a leadership conference at my church that was to begin that evening.

As I got into the car for the trip home, I said to my friend, "If you don't mind, I may take a nap while we travel." She readily agreed that I should do just that. But as I closed my eyes, I felt the familiar, yet still awesome presence of the Holy Spirit stir my mind to think on a particular scripture. My Teacher had decided it was time for class.

He told me to look at Romans 12:1-2. Then He talked to me about it. From there we took a journey through other familiar passages, and for the six hours that it took us to drive home, I wrote down what my Teacher told me. Though I had not had my nap, I was more rested when I arrived home than I would have been had I slept.

My husband met me at the car, and I was trembling with excitement. I said, "Honey, God has talked to me all the way down the road. The Word has come alive. I have just received the most beautiful revelation. Things I have studied and heard for years suddenly fit together."

If we are willing to go through the process required to receive revelation, we will never be disappointed in our walk with God. As we yield to the Holy Spirit's prompting and allow Him to tear away the veil of flesh that keeps us from knowing God intimately, we will behold "wondrous things out of Thy law" (Ps. 119:18, AMP). Then we will find our attitudes, actions and priorities transformed by the Living Word who is being unveiled through us as He is being revealed to us.

My beloved is gone down into
his garden, to the beds
of spices, to feed in the
gardens, and to gather lilies.
I am my beloved's, and
my beloved is mine:
he feedeth among the lilies.

Song of Solomon 6:2-3

7

How to
Receive Revelation

Consider the Lilies

After we have understood the prerequisites for receiving divine revelation — allowing the Holy Spirit to fill us and take us through His processes to tear the veil of flesh away; receiving the written Word of God as the basis of all revelation; and reading and hearing the Word so that faith can fill our hearts — there is yet a further obedience required of us to walk in all the revelation of God.

The apostle James declared emphatically that we

should be doers of the Word, and not hearers only (James 1:22). We certainly understand that God meant us to obey the explicit commands of Scripture, such as loving one another and living holy lives. There are some commands in the Word, however, that we might not recognize as readily, yet they will bring wonderful revelation to our hearts when obeyed.

For example, Jesus instructed us to "consider the lilies how they grow" (Luke 12:27). Have you done that? Have you considered the lilies? The word *consider* is defined as "thinking about something carefully with regard to taking some action." To consider lilies as Jesus asked us to do implies much more than simply enjoying the fragrance and beauty of a lovely flower that decorates the church on Easter Sunday. We must understand something about the nature of the lily.

How does a lily grow? What do lilies represent in the Scriptures? Where are they mentioned? Jesus compared their beauty to the glory of Solomon, and He rated them as more beautiful than the splendor of the richest man on earth. Why would Jesus compare a lily to man's highest splendor? Was He simply stating that He preferred the beauty of a lovely creation of God to the king's riches?

Or was He making a significant comparison between man's glory and the beautiful lily, using picture language that we could only understand by revelation, much as He did when teaching His parables? After searching the Scriptures to see how the lily is mentioned, I realized it is an excellent example to demonstrate how revelation unfolds "hidden" commands of the Word.

The Lily in Scripture

The Bridegroom in the Song of Solomon refers to himself as the lily of the valley and to his bride as a lily among thorns, comparing her to the daughters of Jerusalem. Later in this lovely poetic type of Christ and the church, the Bridegroom is described by his bride as one who feeds among the lilies and who goes down to the garden to gather lilies (Song 2:16; 6:2).

The daughters of Jerusalem are curious about the passion of the Shulamite bride for her Bridegroom and even ask where he is so that they might seek him too (Song 6:1). Yet there is a clear distinction between their relationship to him and that of the bride-to-be. His bride declares that she belongs to him and he to her, and she cannot be dissuaded from seeking him until she finds him.

How the Lily Grows

A brief "consideration" of the natural characteristics of the lily reveals to us that it grows on a single stalk, undivided in its efforts to provide a channel of nutrients to its lovely flower. The Scriptures warn us that "a double minded man is unstable in all his ways" (James 1:8). Jesus instructed us to be single-eyed so that our bodies would be full of light (Luke 11:34).

Because a lily opens its petals early in the morning to receive its daily nourishment from the dew, it is not easily contaminated by the pollution of its immediate environment. Dew is mentioned many times in Scripture and is a symbol of the presence of the Holy Spirit (Ps. 133:3). As believers, we need to open our hearts early each day to receive the fresh dew of the Spirit on our lives and avoid the contamination of the world.

The lily grows deep roots that turn toward the fountainhead of the water source by which it is planted. The apostle Paul instructs us to be "rooted and grounded in love" (Eph. 3:17) telling us that in this way we will know the love of Christ which passes knowledge (v. 19). Becoming deeply rooted in God will bring us to revelation knowledge of Him and provide an ever greater experience of His love in us and for us. As that love is released to others, it will allow them to behold the beauty of the lily and come to the knowledge of God as well.

Even the formation of the lily's lovely petals in groups of five is significant, considering that in Scripture the number five represents grace and redemption.

The lovely white color of many lilies represents the purity of heart and holiness with which the bride must be adorned. The psalmist refers to this heart of holiness when he describes the king's daughter as "all glorious within: her clothing is of wrought gold. She shall be brought unto the king in raiment of needle-work: the virgins her companions that follow her shall be brought unto thee" (Ps. 45:13-14).

Becoming a part of the bride of Christ is not something that occurs automatically; it is the result of a love relationship that is cultivated through single-hearted devotion and drinking of the fountain of life daily. Such a relationship involves a consuming passion for the lover of our souls. Although our acceptance of the Christ of Calvary has not only purchased our salvation but also judicially placed us in position as the bride of Christ, not all believers fit the description of the bride of Christ. As believers we must experientially cultivate the relationship we have with our Bridegroom.

The carefulness of the bride to nurture her relationship with her beloved sheds light on the parable Jesus told about the five foolish and the five wise virgins (see Matt. 25). Those who were *wise* went into the marriage supper while those who were foolish did not. Only those Christians who are single-eyed in their pursuit of a relationship with their divine Bridegroom will experience intimacy with Him. If we see Him as the lover of our souls and pursue our love relationship with Him above all other things of value, we will become prepared for the moment when the bride is presented to the Bridegroom at the great marriage feast in heaven.

There is much we can learn by following Jesus' admonition to consider the lilies of the field, how they grow. We see that Jesus did not come simply to forgive us of our sins and save us from hell, but to restore us to the relationship of single-eyed, wholehearted, purity of love that the Father intended for us when He made mankind.

Many Christians who have accepted Christ as their Savior simply have not entered into a love relationship with Him as their Bridegroom, a relationship which results in the purity of heart and singleness of mind manifested by the passion of the bride. Surely Jesus was expressing His great desire for us to consider these things when He turned our attention to the lily and declared, "Solomon in all his glory was not arrayed like one of these" (Luke 12:27).

Jesus assured us that we can enjoy the rest and

111

repose of the lily, which neither toils nor spins. The beauty of the lily is not dependent on its own efforts. Jesus' promise shows our Savior's great love and watchfulness over our lives. He focuses our hearts, declaring that we should not seek the natural things of the world, but rather the kingdom of God to attain to divine beauty. He promises us that as we seek the kingdom of God, all the things we need will be added to us (Luke 12:27-32).

As we pause to obey Jesus' simple command to "consider the lilies," we can reflect on our own lives to see if the rare beauty of the lily is seen in us. Remembering that to *consider* means to "regard carefully with a view to action," we may see some areas in our lives that need to be adjusted.

Perhaps it is our focus that needs to be adjusted in order to become single-eyed or our consecration in order to receive daily the dew of heaven. Perhaps we are anxiously acquiring "things" without truly seeking the kingdom of God first. Whatever keeps us from pursuing our Bridegroom wholeheartedly will result in great loss to our souls. Becoming rooted and grounded in His love will assure our ultimate heart satisfaction.

Growing Like the Lily

I am sensing in my spirit that the body of Christ must grow up. We are to become sons with knowledge — not in eternity, but now — to be able to do what God has ordained us to do on the earth. We are joint heirs with Christ, destined to sit with Him and rule and reign with Him. But there is more to our callings than having dominion over powers and principalities. We are called to be prepared for the return of our Bridegroom. Some have been entrusted with the ministry of preparing the bride for the Bridegroom.

If only those who *choose* to become a part of the bride of Christ *will* be, it seems that not every born-again person will be a part. Many who have accepted Christ as their Savior have not cultivated an intimate relationship with Him.

Of course, everyone who has been cleansed from sin by the blood of Christ and who is walking in the light will spend eternity with Him. But there are many who know Him only as their Savior. They have stopped on the first step and have gone no further. Others know Him as both Savior and Baptizer and are satisfied. They haven't matured enough even to desire to know Him as their Bridegroom.

The bride of Christ is a divine relationship, not a position. It is a relationship of maturity. The Scriptures teach that when we see Christ, we will be known of Him as we know Him (1 Cor. 13:12). If we know Him only as the Savior and Giver of spiritual blessings and gifts, that is who He will be to us. Though that is wonderful, there is more to relationship with God than gifts and blessings.

In the Old Testament picture of the tabernacle, there was an outer court which led to the holy place, which in turn led to the holy of holies. Though much religious activity happened in the outer court and the holy place, the presence of God was experienced in power only in the holy of holies. Likewise, there are differences in the relationships God has with a babe in Christ, a young adult in Christ and a mature saint in Christ.

With maturity comes the desire as well as the capacity for marriage. When believers fall in love with Jesus, their affections and interests change focus from "things" to a Person. Rather than seeking things that He can give them, they seek the kingdom of God first. Jesus becomes preeminent in their hearts and lives. The highest, greatest aspiration of mature believers is to be able to commune with Christ as their Bridegroom.

True worship in spirit and truth belongs to the mature. It is the immature who are continually coming to the Lord with their lists of requests for blessings and petitions. Though there is always a place for petitioning our Lord, there is also a divine place of pouring out our lives and hearts in worship before Him without asking for anything.

For love of Jesus, a woman broke an alabaster box and poured its costly ointment on the feet of Jesus, to the disgust of those around her. It was a true act of worship that Jesus said would be mentioned wherever the gospel was preached (see Matt. 26:7-13).

Worship, that intimate relationship of the bride with the Bridegroom, is not something we read in the Scriptures like, "Ye must be born-again." It is not apparent in Scripture to the eyes of the natural man or to the babe in Christ. It is one of those truths that must be dug out as silver is mined. It is hidden in the Book for those eyes that are opened to see it. Yet worship is also the spirit of the entire Book. Seeing our relationship to our Bridegroom restored through worship is the Father's deepest desire.

In Genesis, the book of beginnings, we see a beautiful picture of the kind of love relationship we are to have with Jesus. Eliezar, Abraham's servant, was instructed to find a bride for Isaac among God's chosen people — Abraham's own people. Eliezar would know her because she would be at a well drinking water. And she would give not only Eliezar water, but his camels as well (see Gen. 24).

In this very first book of Scripture, Rebekah, the chosen bride for Isaac, is a picture which reveals the nature and character of the bride whom Christ will have from among His people. She will be willing to serve a stranger and will consecrate herself to leave her people in order to become the bride of the one who had sent her such beautiful gifts.

Such character is a result of maturity and cannot be expected of those who have known only Christ as their Savior. Rebekah's life held the fragrance of the lily that was single-eyed and sustained by the dew from heaven. And she was rewarded with the love of her Bridegroom for whom she had left all that was dear to her.

Revelation of the Bridegroom

I cannot express the overwhelming awe I felt the first time I came into the presence of Jesus in such a way that I heard Him say to me, "I love you." I had come into a revelation of worship, and I had learned to be comfortable saying to Him, "I love you, Lord." But for the infinite, almighty, eternal, triune God, the Savior of the world, to come to this creature of dust and say. "Do you know that I love You?" — it seemed like a dream. I was filled with an indescribable peace and sense of well-being, a feeling of being loved in the ultimate essence of love.

When Jesus first came to me in an open vision as I

was alone in prayer, I looked into His eyes and saw His broad shoulders and flowing hair. It was as though the golden glow of glory were shining through His hair. His features were so strong as He came and stood in front of me. He said to me, "I want you to be mine. If you will give Me your body, I will bless it."

I wept and said to Him, "It belongs to my husband."

He replied gently, "Give it to Me, and I will bless it and give it back to him. Then I will teach you how you can share My love, and I can be the sweetheart of your spirit and soul." I felt His arms around me, and He talked to me about my walk and my life and said, "I don't want your lips to be lips of leprosy."

I asked Him, "How did my lips become leprous?"

He said, "Adam took the forbidden fruit and ate of the words of Satan. As a result his mouth became leprous, and the human family was born with leprous lips [a type of sin]." Our lips speak lies, they exaggerate and brag to impress people, they speak in anger and utter profanity. Our lips are leprous until we get into the presence of the Bridegroom, and His words fall from our lips (see Song 4:11). When we hear Him say, "Go and sin no more," and "Arise, take up thy bed and walk," our hearts are changed.

Only as we focus our hearts and minds on our Bridegroom can we expect to have His fragrance imparted to us. It is worth the complete consecration of our lives in every aspect to know Him intimately. There is nothing to be sought on this earth that is higher than a relationship with Christ as the Lover of our souls.

We can be single-eyed as we look to Him — shutting everything else out when we stand in His presence, look into His eyes and hear His words. Then we will be a part of the bride of Christ when He comes. He is not going to be married to strangers. He is looking for those who love Him.

The Shulamite told the daughters of Jerusalem that the Bridegroom had gone down into the garden to feed and to gather lilies. How could we summarize the lilies' growth? They grow in purity, tall and straight, dependent on Him, with leaves that are fresh and green, and with a fragrance about them that greets everyone who touches them. They do not strive, but with single-eyed focus they grow toward the light, revealing a beauty that is unparalleled by man's greatest adornments.

May the world know us, the bride of Christ, as a lovely bed of lilies.

The lily is only one example of the many word pictures contained in the Scriptures that can unlock precious revelatory truths to our hearts if we will obey the divine injunction to "consider." It is no wonder that the Lord told Joshua to meditate day and night on the book of the law and observe to do according to all that was written (Josh. 1:8). In meditating on the Word and being obedient to God's commands we give the Holy Spirit access to our hearts. He can then fill our minds with the revelatory truths that will transform us and unveil the Christ within us.

Study to show thyself approved unto God, a workman that needeth not to be ashamed, rightly dividing the word of truth.

2 Timothy 2:15

8

Hindrances and Helps to Receiving Revelation

Learning to Read "Out"

Even sincere, born-again Christians have many times read a wrong meaning into a verse of Scripture because of their church theology, prejudice or cultural bias. I call this "reading into" the Scriptures what was not intended instead of "reading out" what the Holy Spirit actually wrote.

For example, I can now use the same scriptures to teach the validity of the baptism of the Holy Spirit and His gifts as I used before to teach against praying in tongues. We too often read into a verse what others have taught us that it means — something that fits their doctrinal position.

After I was healed and baptized in the Holy Spirit with the evidence of speaking in other tongues, having previously believed that neither experience was valid for today, I took my Bible and sat at the feet of Jesus and asked, "What else do I not understand, Lord?" The value of my theological degrees and doctrinal positions was shattered in a moment of time when the Holy Spirit revealed Himself to me as my Healer and Baptizer.

We have read into the Book and built our own doctrines, theologies and philosophies based on our Western culture, our unbelief, our prejudices and other faulty criteria. My Bible professors taught me to interpret the Scriptures according to certain doctrinal positions, and I missed the truth of healing and the baptism of the Holy Spirit along with many other truths. I almost died, literally, because of my lack of revelation regarding the promises for healing in the Word.

By the mercy of God and as a result of others' fervent prayers for my healing and baptism in the Spirit, I have had the joy of teaching the Word for many years with new revelation and understanding.

Before my healing I was a sincere theologian, believing with all my heart what I had been taught. I had looked at my dying daddy and told him that miracles were not for today. Why? Because that was what I had been taught. Our doctrinal position declared that because that which was perfect was come (the Word), we did not need the gifts of the Holy Spirit. (The doctrine comes from an erroneous interpretation of 1 Corinthians 13 and is a view still held by many.) If God had not sovereignly healed me from a fatal disease, I would have gone to my grave without believing that God can and does heal today.

This is only one example of wrong theology which has kept many believers from a true revelation of God and His Word. Unless we allow the Holy Spirit to interpret the Scriptures for us, we can never come to a true understanding of them.

Besides wrong doctrine, there are five great hindrances to receiving revelation that rob our churches and our personal lives of true knowledge of God.

Five Major Hindrances

I have anticipated, preached, proclaimed and believed for the next move of God in which we will see the great revival and the subsequent glorious harvest of souls. As I have waited expectantly, the Holy Spirit has deeply impressed upon me that the church must be delivered from areas of wrong thinking which obstruct and hinder the revelation of God to our hearts and keep us from this great visitation of God.

When I refer to the church, I do not mean an organization, location or institution, but the living organism of the body of Christ — the church of which Christ is the Head. The church for which Jesus is returning needs to be cleansed from at least five hindering concepts in order to be a part of the coming great revival.

Denominationalism

Denominationalism is one of the hindrances. A

denomination is simply defined as "a class or society of individuals supporting a system of principles and called by the same name." As long as a denomination remains only a vehicle through which to carry the life of Jesus, it is not harmful. It can be an instrument of God. However, when it serves as a vehicle for promoting denominational doctrines which are taught with dogmatic finality, it dangerously limits greater streams of truth that would flow into it and often produces legalism. When that happens, the vehicle needs to be parked, and its divine Occupant allowed to come forth unhindered.

The purpose of denominations is similar to that of the scaffolding that is necessary during a building process. Scaffolding was not designed to obscure the structure permanently. Once the building is completed, it needs to be removed in order for the real building to be seen. Denominationalism is a human structure established upon ideologies and dogmas that often obscures the true church Christ is building. For the life of Christ to be seen in the church, the scaffolding of man's denominationalism must be removed.

Traditions of Men

Second, the church must be delivered from the *traditions of men*. Webster's defines a tradition as "an inherited or established pattern of thought or behavior; the handing down of information and beliefs by word of mouth or by example from one generation to another without written instruction."

The Pharisees asked Jesus, "Why do thy disciples transgress the tradition of the elders? for they wash not their hands when they eat bread" (Matt. 15:2). Their traditions were more important to them than the Word of God. Jesus leveled severe criticism at, and even directly repudiated the oral tradition by concluding that the oral decrees of the elders were wholly of human origin (Mark 7:6-13).

Paul declared that he was exceedingly zealous of the traditions of his fathers until "it pleased God...to reveal his Son in me" (Gal. 1:15-16). He was delivered from devout loyalty to an intense religious system when Christ was revealed in him.

Unfortunately, in the church today man's carnal mind has interpreted many of the scriptures for us, not allowing the Holy Spirit, the divine Teacher who wrote the Book, to reveal its truth to our spirits. As a result, we have developed religious practices which have become comfort zones to our church mentality. We have failed to rightly divide the Word of God, reading it instead according to the instruction of men.

Peter reminded the Christians that they were not redeemed with corruptible things such as silver and gold "from your futile way of life inherited from your forefathers" (1 Pet. 1:18, NAS). The church must return to the Word of God and allow the Spirit of truth to teach us and deliver us from the religious tradition that has become, in man's eyes, a higher law than God's Word. Irrespective of man's laws and traditions, God's Word is the final "yea and amen."

Prejudice

Prejudice is a third area of thinking from which the church must be delivered. Unreasonable biases, judgments or opinions that are contrary to facts, and that breed suspicion, intolerance or hatred have no place in Christ's church. Whether our prejudice is against race, gender, sect, class, status or another area, it will keep us from hearing and receiving the truth of God as revealed by the Holy Spirit.

Paul not only declared that "after that faith [in Christ] is come" (Gal. 3:25) our prejudicial distinctions do not exist (v. 28), but he also wrote to Timothy to "observe these things without preferring one before another, doing nothing by partiality" (1 Tim. 5:21). Christ's true church will be free from the destructive power of prejudice.

Culture

Perhaps nothing is more basic to our natural thinking than *culture*. Those concepts, habits, skills, arts, institutions and refinements of thought, emotion, manners and taste which characterize our native culture seem "right" to us. For that reason, missionaries have often exported more of their culture than of the Christ life.

We have to be delivered from our bondage to culture in order to understand other cultures and allow the Christ in us to move in and through any culture. He brings a new and higher way of life that transcends the limitations of culture. Our Lord can live in any culture that will surrender its ways to Him.

Though most of us would have difficulty relating to African tribal cultures, it is a fact that thousands of precious African people are receiving Jesus every day. After they are saved, these African Christians will find that they cannot continue serving a witchdoctor or offering blood sacrifices and practicing other tribal customs. They will have to come to know Christ as the One who meets all their needs. He will free them from the ungodly practices of their culture in the same way He frees people in western cultures from their ungodly practices.

Customs

Finally, the church must be delivered from *customs.* Legally, a custom refers to any long-established, uniform practice that is accepted by common consent of a society to such an extent that, though unwritten, it has taken on the force of the law. Customs are enforced by social disapproval of any violation.

Christ has freed men from the tyranny of man's standard of righteousness which comes from without by imposition, and He has put within us His standard of righteousness, which comes by the Holy Spirit. The Spirit writes God's laws upon our hearts. Paul denounced the Jews, who were trying to add their customs as requirements for salvation. By the imposition of these requirements, they implied that the sacrificial, vicarious, efficacious death of Christ was not quite enough to effect salvation (Gal. 2:21).

Wherever the church has inadvertently included the demands of custom as criteria for the Christ life, it must repent and return to complete faith in the work of Calvary.

The customs of my religious background dictated that women were not allowed to cut their hair or to wear jewelry. These practices were considered sinful according to my denomination's interpretation of the Scriptures. To violate these customs would bring the wrath of the church upon a woman.

I have been set free from the bondage of these customs, realizing that they were a result of man-made laws which were trying to legislate holiness. I have learned that holiness is a matter of the heart. If our hearts are holy, our appearances will demonstrate modesty and godliness — without the stricture of man-made customs.

Only as we allow the Holy Spirit to speak truth to us, convicting our hearts and cleansing us of our wrong thinking in any of the five areas discussed above, will we be able to receive revelation from the Word of God and be prepared to be a part of the great coming revival. Even the most basic revelation of spiritual life in God is not possible as long as we are taught to understand the Scriptures through faulty perspectives.

Examples of Commonly Misinterpreted Scriptures

I know the following paragraphs may challenge you to look at some Scriptures differently than you have in the past. Most of us have read the Scriptures with the mind-set of our western culture. Without understanding the customs of Jesus' day, we cannot always understand the significance of certain events. Please allow the Holy Spirit to open your minds to the possibility of a different perspective as we study these passages. Pray for God's illuminating light to bring fresh revelation to you as you read.

Misunderstanding the woman at the well. All of us who have taught that the Samaritan woman Jesus addressed at the well was an adulteress will have to repent to her on the great judgment day (see John 4).

In all of Jesus' dialogue with this woman, He did not mention sin. Though He told her the history of her life, He did not intimate that she was living in sin. We deduced that she was because we did not understood the customs of the day.

A Jewish rabbi explained the fallacy of our interpretation of this passage of Scripture to me. The law of the day allowed a woman who was widowed to marry her deceased husband's brother. He was responsible to raise up seed for his brother. Apparently, the Samaritan woman had been widowed five times and was engaged to the sixth brother. The custom of the day did not allow a Jewish or Samaritan woman to speak to a man on the street. But after she had married five brothers, she was allowed to speak to men, and men were allowed to speak to her.

It is a Jewish custom also that when a woman is betrothed to a man, she is brought to the groom's home before marriage, not to consummate the relationship, but to take on the family traits. For this reason Jesus said to her, "He whom thou now hast is not thy husband" (John 4:18).

According to our Western mind, to "have" a man who is not your husband means you are involved in an adulterous relationship. Not so in the Jewish tradition. It simply refers to a time of betrothal.

My Jewish rabbi friend explained this custom to me and asked if I thought Ruth the Moabitess was an adulteress. I responded vehemently, "Of course not." Yet she did sleep at the feet of Boaz before they were married. That was what she was instructed to do by Naomi, and following her mother-in-law's suggestion in no way violated moral law.

The Samaritan woman called Jesus a prophet because He knew she had been married to five brothers, not because He had discovered her life of sin. There was no mention of sin. The subject of their conversation was worship.

The greatest truth revealed through the encounter with the woman at the well is that God seeks people to worship Him in spirit and in truth (John 4:23). That requires revelation by the Holy Spirit to our spirits, taking us from religious questions regarding where we should worship, such as the Samaritan woman asked, to an encounter with the living God, which she unknowingly had. She realized that Jesus was a prophet, and when she returned to her city, her zeal indicated that she had received revelation of God. She became an effective evangelist because of her encounter with Jesus.

Were there nine unthankful lepers? Most of us have heard and many of us have taught a sermon on the nine unthankful men from the account of Jesus healing ten lepers (Luke 17:12-19).We have taught that the nine did not come back to Jesus because they were not thankful. Is that really what the Book teaches? When we understand Old Testament law, we realize that is not the case.

Someone has said quite accurately that the New Testament is in the Old concealed, and the Old Testament is in the New revealed. The seed of New Testament revelation is hidden in types and shadows in the Old Testament. The New Testament is a fulfillment of all that the Old Testament foreshadowed. So we must be careful to interpret the New Testament without violating truths established in the Old Testament.

In the case of the ten lepers, we need to understand the Old Testament law concerning the leper to interpret correctly this passage. The answer to why the nine lepers did not return is in the Old Testament. These ten lepers came crying, "Jesus, Master, have mercy on us" (Luke 17:13). The fact that they called Jesus "Master" shows that they were submitted to the King. It means they were willing to do whatever He told them. When Jesus saw them, the only thing He said to them was, "Go shew yourselves unto the priests" (v. 14).

Why did Jesus send them to the priests? The lepers were sent to the priests because the law of the leper written in chapter 13 of Leviticus declared that people with leprosy could not return to the camp without first being examined by the priests. There was a two-week waiting period to confirm their healing during which the lepers was confined to a certain place (Lev. 13:4-5). When the priests declared that they were healed, they could go home. So Jesus kept the law in every point.

The Scriptures declare that the one leper who returned to give thanks to Jesus was a Samaritan. Since Samaritans were not subject to Jewish law, this man would not have been able to receive a health certificate from the priests. He was free to come back, while the other nine were shut up awaiting confirmation of their healing by the priests. When they received that, they could go home, not having to cry "Unclean" anymore. The lepers went as Jesus told them to and received their healing as they went. What faith!

But the Samaritan had no one to give him a health certificate. So he came back to Jesus, his priest, to give thanks. Jesus asked, "Were there not ten cleansed? but where are the nine? There are not found that returned to give glory to God, save this stranger" (Luke 17:17-18).

We have misunderstood Jesus' statement that they could not be found to give thanks. They were shut up according to Old Testament law and could not return to give thanks. The Scriptures do not say anything about their being unthankful. They were simply not available to return to Jesus, except for the Samaritan who came to Jesus as his priest. Jesus' question, "Were there not ten cleansed? but where are the nine?" was not so much an expression of surprise as a matter-of-fact report about the event of healing. He knew that even as He asked the question, the nine healed lepers were presenting themselves as evidence of the miracle that took place. Can you imagine the surprise the priests must have felt?

Was Thomas doubting? The Holy Spirit told me I would have to apologize to Thomas for calling him doubting Thomas. I have already repented by faith. I am sorry I have said negative things about him.

There is a most beautiful revelation of the new birth in the incident that involves Thomas and the appearance of the resurrected Christ. On the day of the resurrection Jesus appeared to the disciples in the upper room. Ten of the twelve disciples were present. Of course, Judas Iscariot was not there. For some reason Thomas was not there.

After greeting the disciples who were present, Jesus breathed on them and said, "Receive ye the Holy Ghost" (John 20:22). He opened their eyes and their understanding. He showed them his hands and His side (John 20:20). He invited them to touch his body (Luke 24:39). They became recipients of the efficacious, vicarious, substitutionary work of Calvary that day. They were breathed upon by God. Jesus also commissioned them, saying, "As my Father hath sent me, even so send I you" (v. 21).

Thomas wasn't there that day, so the other disciples told him about their encounter with the risen Christ. They had personally touched Him and been touched by Him, receiving the life and commission He gave them when He said, "Receive ye the Holy Ghost." When Thomas responded, "Except I shall see in his hands the print of the nails, and put my finger into the print of the nails, and thrust my hand into his side, I will not believe," he was making a plea to have the same encounter the other disciples had had (John 20:25). He wanted personally to touch Him as they had done. The fact is, we don't get saved by proxy, but by a personal encounter with the living Christ. Thomas wanted that for himself.

Eight days later when Jesus appeared to the disciples again, Thomas was there. After Jesus allowed Thomas to touch His wounds, Jesus commended him for believing. The response of Thomas is a graphic demonstration of the requirements of the new birth — a personal encounter with Christ. God showed us by example that if we don't touch Him for ourselves, our spirits will not be opened to receive His breath.

Helps to Receiving Revelation

We must be aware of hindrances to receiving revelation from the Word so that we can be cleansed from them or avoid them. But we also need to understand the many helps to overcoming those hindrances so we can enjoy a revelatory relationship with our Lord.

Ignorance is often one of the enemy's most effective weapons against us — keeping us from knowing the truth that will set us free. Since the beginning of time, God has been using many means to reveal Himself to man to help us overcome our ignorance of Him and His ways.

God Reveals Himself as God

It is our Father's greatest desire to reveal Himself to mankind. The entire plan of redemption testifies to this fact.

The omnipotent God has from the beginning been unfolding His will to restore mankind to relationship with Himself. He has been initiating ways to reveal Himself and His character to man, recording them carefully in the Book of the Law for all to read. He has used three major ways to communicate His love — the revelation of His great heart — to mankind.

1. His Names

There are several hundred names of God recorded in the Old Testament. Each one reveals a beautiful aspect of His character. To Moses, God revealed Himself as the "I AM." To Abraham on Mount Moriah, He revealed Himself as Jehovah-Jireh, the God who provides. A comprehensive study of the names of God in the Scriptures will reveal to our hearts an understanding of who God is.

2. His Acts

God also reveals Himself to us through the things He does. He revealed His power to the Israelites by dividing the waters of the Red Sea. He revealed His authority and code of righteousness when He wrote the law of God on tablets of stone. He displayed His judgments when He sent the flood in Noah's day and later burned the cities of Sodom and Gomorrah. He showed His mercy in the promise of the rainbow and the answering of the cry of Abraham for his nephew Lot.

Every time the hand of God is seen in His dealings with mankind, a portion of His divine nature is revealed.

3. Descriptions of Himself

Every description of God by those who were writing under the inspiration of the Holy Spirit gives us wonderful revelation of who God is. Especially descriptive are the psalms of David and others, revealing God as our shield and buckler and our high tower for protection (Ps. 35:2; 144:2).

One of my favorite portraits of God is the Shepherd of Psalm 23. Entire books have been written to help us understand the significance of God as our Shepherd. Yet, He is also described in the Word as a consuming fire and the Judge of the whole earth (Heb. 12:29; Ps. 50:6). Every description of Him reveals a facet of His character by which we come to know Him.

It is a simple fact that we can know God as deeply as we want to know Him. Too often we do not take the responsibility of seeking Him, of trying to gain an understanding of His names, His acts and His descriptions of Himself so that revelation can enlighten our hearts. Sometimes we simply want God to visit us, to come to us and make us feel good.

But unless we allow the Word of God to define Him for us, unless we seek to know every facet of His character, we will not know Him intimately. In order to bring the treasures of Himself to our lives, we must seek for Him as one digs for silver.

When we start to dig, sitting down to study the Word, we need to be sure to invite our Teacher to the class. We need to ask the Holy Spirit to give us the revelation we need. There is no use studying without Him because our natural minds won't understand what we are reading. I often pray the prayer of Ephesians 1, asking for "the spirit of wisdom and revelation in the knowledge of Him" (v. 17).

A Revelation of Salvation

I had been born-again for twenty years before I understood what really happened to me in my conversion experience. I had taught the Word without a real revelation of what salvation involved. After I was healed and baptized in the Holy Spirit, and as my Teacher began to explain the Book to me, He asked me if I wanted Him to explain the impartation of the living seed.

I was so embarrassed. I said, "Jesus, you mean I don't even know that? I have been preaching for so long, and I don't even know what happened to me when I got saved! I am going back to first base for sure."

He comforted me by saying, "Daughter, you don't tell your children about the birds and bees when they are babies. Now you are old enough for Me to tell you what happened to you in the new birth."

He showed me the little virgin Mary kneeling before the Lord. As I saw the Holy Spirit overshadowing her, I understood that in the same way that He had overshadowed Mary, He had overshadowed my spirit when I was born again. Just as He had impregnated her with Jesus, He had impregnated me by placing the incorruptible seed of God in my spirit. The reality of salvation is that God is living in our spirits from the moment we are born again.

Deeper Understanding of the Word

On another occasion when I was meditating on His Word, the Holy Spirit brought to mind what God declared through the prophet Isaiah: "So shall my word be that goeth forth out of my mouth: it shall not return unto me void, but it shall accomplish that which I please, and it shall prosper in the thing whereto I sent it" (Is. 55:11). I had understood this verse to mean that whatever God spoke would come to pass, and that when His Word was preached, there would be results — it would not return void of fruitfulness.

The Holy Spirit did not chide me for my interpretation, implying that it was valid as far as it went. But He asked me these questions: Who is the Word? Where did He come from? To what place did He return?

My mind immediately went to the first chapter of the gospel of John, and I answered that the Word was Jesus. "In the beginning was the Word, and the Word was with God, and the Word was God" (v. 1). I also remembered the verse in Philippians that says Jesus "thought it not robbery to be equal with God" (2:6).

Yet He emptied Himself of His deity and became a man and a servant of men, becoming obedient unto death, even death on a cross. When He ascended after His resurrection from the dead, He returned to His Father.

As the Holy Spirit opened my understanding, I realized that the prophet Isaiah was declaring that Christ, the Living Word, will not return to His Father empty — void. The church will go back to the Father in Him. The Word came to earth to retrieve the church, and He will return filled with all born-again believers. The Living Word will accomplish everything the Father intended to be accomplished.

What a beautiful dimension of the Word came to my heart with this revelation. Not only does the Holy Spirit correct our faulty understanding of some scriptures, but He also adds to our limited understanding of others.

God has made our requirement for coming to know Him very clear throughout the Scriptures. To know Him we must seek Him and His kingdom above all else. The effort required on our part will be rewarded with the divine treasure of the revelation of God Himself. Love for God will motivate us to seek Him until we find Him whom our soul loves.

Jesus declared, "Blessed are they which do hunger and thirst after righteousness: for they shall be filled" (Matt. 5:6). Hunger for God is a wonderful condition that will bring eternal benefits to our souls. Christian books and tapes may be helpful to us, but they can never substitute for the personal digging for silver that brings a revelation of God to our souls.

———— ❀ ————

Yea, if thou criest after knowledge, and liftest up thy voice for understanding; If thou seekest her as silver, and searchest for her as for hid treasures; Then shalt thou understand the fear of the Lord, and find the knowledge of God.

Proverbs 2:3-5

9

Digging for Silver

Practical Tools for the Task

If in your reading to this point you have been inspired to seek fresh revelation of God, you are ready for some very practical guidelines and methods for mining this precious silver. Here some will undoubtedly falter, preferring to gaze at the beauty of the silver others have rather than picking up the tools and exerting the effort required to dig for themselves.

Though it is true, as we have seen, that it is the work of the Holy Spirit to unveil the divine life of

Christ within us, it is also true that we must make ourselves available to His working by filling our minds with the Word of God.

At first, the tools may seem useless for mining the priceless treasure — the beautiful revelation of God we have been contemplating. But without these practical instruments to help us, we will not be successful in extracting the precious silver ore of wisdom and revelation for our own souls. We dare not be satisfied with the revelation of another, for it will not have the same power to redeem our souls that a personal revelation of God has.

Digging Tools

My daddy had quite an elaborate workshop in our home, with many expensive and sophisticated tools which qualified him to do difficult carpentry, plumbing and electrical home improvement tasks. But he also had a small toolbox that he carried with him everywhere. He was never without it.

As a little girl, tagging behind my daddy, I learned to identify the tools in that little box. I even learned to use some of the most-often needed and most-easily used.

While we do not need an elaborate workshop such as a theologian's library to study God's Word effectively, we do need to have a toolbox filled with basic items that will help us in our study.

The Scriptures describe the practical work involved in digging for silver when they admonish us to "Study to shew thyself approved unto God, a workman that needeth not to be ashamed, rightly dividing the word of truth" (2 Tim. 2:15). If we aren't willing to apply ourselves to the work of study, we don't want wisdom badly enough. We need to ask God for a greater hunger for Himself.

A Place of Study

In this world of electronic noise in which telephones, radios, TVs and CDs are creating a constant barrage of sound in our offices, homes and cars, we need to think seriously about preparing a place for study which will afford us the quiet we need to "Be still and know that I am God." We need a place where we can effectively limit the interruptions of clients, family, pets and unsolicited phone calls.

Our place of study should be comfortable and should include a desk (or table) and writing utensils for taking notes, as well as shelves for storing study books. The necessary tools for digging for silver should be conveniently placed so we don't have to run to the basement or upstairs to locate something we need. Since we are careful to make places for our children, our pets and even our memorabilia, how much more should we take care to prepare a suitable place to seek God and to furnish it with all the necessary tools.

The Bible

A prerequisite for Bible study is a good study Bible. It should be one with print that can be easily read and with paper that is suitable for marking.

I find the King James Version unsurpassed for its beauty of expression in the English language. However, other translations are necessary as well, particularly in view of language changes. A reading of various modern translations will help to throw light on many Bible passages.

A word of caution should be observed here. Translations cannot be easily evaluated. Some translators have allowed their theological bias to enter into their translating work. For this reason it is wise to anchor our reading in the King James Version and to use other versions as supplements, referring to the original languages if possible when questions are raised regarding translation. Other useful translations, each having their own study helps, include the following:

Thompson Chain Reference Bible. This thorough and helpful work has a host of notes in the margin and an excellent section of "Condensed Encyclopedia" divided into more than four thousand topics. It also contains information on the canon and the principal English versions, an outlined analysis of each book, a number of maps, a concordance and an index. This Bible also has a good harmony of the four gospels and several excellent charts.

Dickson Analytical Edition (Word Bible Company). This Bible contains a dictionary, concordance, topical study section, chronology outlines and outstanding facts about each book, as well as information on the canon and various versions. References are footnoted below each verse, and textual revisions are bracketed in the verses.

New King James Bible. Many believe this translation is the nearest to the original transcripts of the Bible.

The New Jerusalem translation is esteemed by many as well. Several other reference Bibles could be mentioned, such as the *New Oxford Reference Bible,* the

Holman Study Bible and the *New American Standard* version.

The Worrell New Testament with notes by the translator, A. S. Worrell. This is published by the Gospel Publishing House of Springfield, Missouri, and is footnoted with many helpful alternative renderings and explanatory notes.

The Englishman's Bible by Thomas Newberry. This Bible has been a blessing to many. It has marks and signs meant to give the ordinary English reader the full sense of the original Hebrew and Greek. The maps and charts of the tabernacle and temple, with explanatory notes, are valuable.

The Emphasized Bible by Joseph Bryant Rotherham. This Bible, particularly sections containing Old Testament notes, is useful as a study and reference book.

The Moffatt Bible translation. This one has many brilliant insights, but the liberal theology of the author shows on occasion.

New Testament in Modern Speech by Richard Weymouth. This translation is clear, simple, dignified and sound from a doctrinal viewpoint.

Goodspeed's translation. This Bible tends to be on the side of liberalism.

William's translation. This work is valuable, particularly in the translation of the Greek tenses.

Montgomery's translation. This Bible has been rated by some as one of the finer modern translations.

The New Testament in Modern English by J. B. Phillips. This work, a paraphrase, is picturesque. Its low-keyed prose is almost casual. For example, the familiar King James "holy kiss" (as in 1 Cor. 16:20) becomes "shake hands all around."

The New Testament: An Expanded Translation is an interpretive translation, as is the *Amplified Bible*. Both are considered sound and helpful for study purposes.

Reading the same passage of Scripture from different translations can shed light on the passage's true meaning as we ask the Holy Spirit to unveil the divine message it contains. Although it is good to follow a daily reading schedule, it is not necessary to devour large portions of the Scripture at a time. Many times the Holy Spirit will illuminate one word in a passage, and it becomes beneficial to search out that word in other passages. Learning to follow the leadership of the Holy Spirit in our Bible study will always lead us to the richest veins of silver.

The Concordance

One of the foremost tools for Bible study is the concordance. It provides immediate access to any scripture verse, even if one remembers only one word or a few words contained in it.

Three concordances are recognized leaders in the field: *Cruden's Unabridged Concordance, Young's Analytical Concordance to the Bible* (311,000 separate references to words and phrases in the Bible), and *Strong's Exhaustive Concordance*. The latter two are more comprehensive.

The Englishman's Greek Concordance of the New Testament and *The Englishman's Hebrew and Chaldee Concordance of the Old Testament*, along with a Greek lexicon and Hebrew lexicon, can be of great value for more advanced studies by Bible students. Personal preferences vary as to which concordance is best. A concordance helps greatly to

144

develop an understanding of a line of truth in the Bible.

Helpful Word Studies

The Complete Word Study Dictionary (New Testament), by Spiros Zodhiates, (1992) published by AMG Publishers of Chattanooga, Tennessee, is a wonderful tool for getting the serious student to study the words in the original languages. AMG has also published *The Complete Word Study Dictionary: New Testament*, which gives invaluable help in the digging of silver.

Bible Dictionaries and Encyclopedias

Another very important aid to Bible study is a dictionary of the Bible. Like any dictionary, it is an alphabetically arranged compilation of words and their definitions. A Bible dictionary contains words with biblical significance. Included are proper nouns — the names of persons and places — as well as common nouns with scriptural meanings.

Through the use of a dictionary and an encyclopedia, the student can obtain a clearer understanding of difficult words and unfamiliar names of persons, places and things. For example, the cubit, a biblical unit of measure, is found to be nearly eighteen inches. The word *penny* is discovered to be the translation of the Greek word denarius, which was the chief Roman silver coin, worth about fifteen to seventeen cents, or the equivalent of a day's wages in Jesus' time.

In a Bible dictionary, the common noun *stone* is

treated with its particular biblical significance, with references to the places where the word appears. The reader can discover that the *hind* is a deer. The word *publican* is defined as the collector of Roman revenue. A dictionary will give detailed information regarding this class of Romans, hated among the Jews for their fraudulent extraction under the vicious system of government.

The use of a Bible dictionary and encyclopedia will bring a flood of light to the student when looking for the meaning of unfamiliar terms. Among the better known works are *Davis Dictionary of the Bible, Unger's Concise Bible Dictionary, The New Bible Dictionary* by J. D. Douglas, *Smith's Bible Dictionary,* and the new *Pictorial Bible Dictionary* by Merrill C. Tenney.

For those who desire a more exhaustive treatment of subject matter, there is *The International Standard Bible Encyclopedia* in five volumes and the *Dictionary of the Bible* by Sir William Smith in one volume (printed by Thomas Nelson). The *Westminster Concise Bible Dictionary* is one of my favorites to use.

Bible Atlas — Bible History

Though of secondary importance to the basic aids already listed, a Bible atlas or geography, a book on Biblical history and a book on Bible manners and customs can make substantial contributions to the study of the Bible.

A Bible atlas helps the student visualize the setting of great events of Scripture. As a source book of general information on Bible geography, geology and archaeology, an atlas contains colored and outline maps and photographs.

For example, the missionary journeys of Paul as recorded in the book of Acts and the founding of the churches by the apostle, along with his later epistles to the churches, take on enriched meaning to the student who has a knowledge of the geography of the lands involved. The same could be said for the journeys of Jesus, Abraham and other significant Bible personalities.

Baker's Bible Atlas is a good atlas.

A larger work I highly recommend is *The Historical Geography of the Holy Land* by George Smith. The same author has an accompanying *Historical Atlas of the Holy Land.*

Bible manners and customs shed light on the understanding of the Bible as revealed in books such as *The Land and the Book* by Charles Page.

A Bible Handbook

A Bible handbook is a valuable tool for study. It may duplicate information in other types of books and could be used as a substitute by those who do not wish to invest in a number of books. *Halley's Bible Handbook,* as an example, is a mine of general Bible information.

A Topical Textbook

Students of the Bible use to good advantage those books which arrange subjects in topical fashion.

Nave's Topical Bible is a sort of concordance with full texts, a digest of twenty thousand topics and subtopics and one hundred thousand references to the Scriptures. Billy Graham has preferred this Bible for years, both for personal study and for platform ministry.

Commentary

A Bible commentary, as the name suggests, comments on the Bible, passage by passage and verse by verse, interpreting its meaning. For hundreds of years Bible scholars and spiritual leaders have recorded the results of their studies, and much of this has been gathered in various commentaries.

Some commentaries are the work of a single author, while others are a compilation of the efforts of a number of men. Commentaries may range in size from one volume to well over fifty volumes.

Since a commentary is written for the purpose of interpreting Scripture, care should be taken in selecting a set. Three of the better-known concise commentaries are *Matthew Henry's Commentary on the Whole Bible, New Commentary on the Whole Bible* by Jamieson, Fausset and Brown, and *The Wycliffe Bible Commentary.*

My purpose here has been to initiate the sincere believer into a variety of study helps that will serve as effective tools for the serious student of the Word. A number of Bible study tools have been listed and specific titles have been mentioned. However, this list is very limited and does not necessarily give the best title in a given category. Perhaps it will serve as a help to those who are beginning to develop a Bible study library.

For the typical American who enjoys blessings of

convenience items such as microwave ovens, quick-dry nail polish and other timesaving devices, it is important to note that the serious study of the Scriptures will not always be convenient. With all our timesaving devices, we are still the busiest generation that ever lived. It will require sacrifice just to come to the place of study.

Once there, we need to be willing to exert effort in study and prayer in order to reach the rich veins of silver awaiting us in the revelation of the Word of God to our souls. I can only encourage every hungry heart that whatever the sacrifice and effort required, it will be worth it all to savor the presence of God in your soul, which is the only source of true satisfaction we can know.

---- ❖ ----

And be not conformed to this world: but be ye transformed by the renewing of your mind, that ye may prove what is that good, and acceptable, and perfect, will of God.

Romans 12:2

10

Transfiguration: The End of Revelation

Becoming Sons With Knowledge

The idea that we can think Christ's thoughts is almost incomprehensible. Yet Paul declared of us, "We have the mind of Christ" (1 Cor. 2:16). This is true to the extent that we walk in maturity and in divine revelation of the Christ-life within.

God has intended that we all "come in the unity of the faith, and of the knowledge of the Son of God, unto a perfect man, unto the measure of the stature of the fullness of Christ" (Eph. 4:13). To that end He

151

gave gifts to the church — apostles, prophets, evangelists, pastors and teachers — "for the perfecting of the saints, for the work of the ministry, for the edifying of the body of Christ" (Eph. 4:11-12). His goal is to have mature sons (and daughters) who will reflect the love of the Father as Christ did on the earth.

One of the seven offices of the Holy Spirit through which He accomplishes the plan of God is the spirit of adoption. Our Western custom regarding adoption of children is quite different from Eastern custom and has clouded our biblical understanding of adoption.

Our practice of adoption can be defined simply as "to take by choice into relationship." In our culture, adoption involves taking an infant or child from someone else's family, giving him our surname and legally making him our child. We change his environment, and he will undoubtedly adopt many of our characteristics simply by living with us. We can even influence his choices, and he will share our outlook on life and our attitudes about many of life's situations. However, the traits he received by heredity cannot be changed because his bloodline was not affected by adoption.

In Bible culture, adoption did not refer to the practice of taking someone else's infant or child into one's home to raise as one's own. When a son grew to maturity and was equipped to bear the family name responsibly, he was declared by his father to be "a son" and was adopted as an heir of the family estate. Adoption was the recognition of mature sonship (Gal. 4:1-2). It did not take place at birth. The declaration of adoption took place at maturity; it signified heirship and throneship, rulership and joint-ownership.

It is written of Jesus that He "increased in wisdom

and stature, and in favour with God and man" (Luke 2:52). These few words about Jesus' life as a young man reveal the maturing process that prepared Him to be a Son. The prophet Isaiah declared, "For unto us a child is born, unto us a son is given: and the government shall be upon His shoulder" (Is. 9:6). Although Jesus was the incarnate Christ-child born to a virgin, Mary, He was required to grow to maturity to become the Son who "is given."

What was the first thing the Father said audibly about Jesus at His water baptism? He declared from heaven for all to hear, "This is My beloved Son" (Matt. 3:17). His declaration was not just a simple reiteration of Jesus' identity. It meant that Jesus had qualified for sonship in the Father's eyes. He had satisfied the divine requirements for sonship. When Jesus went to the Mount of Transfiguration, God declared again, "This is My beloved Son, in whom I am well pleased" (Matt. 17:5).

Jesus did nothing that the Father did not tell Him to do. He lived to please His Father only. We must follow Jesus' example if we are to be called sons of God. One is not a mature son in the biblical sense who has not absorbed his father's spirit, heart, vision and purpose, desiring to please him in all things. That maturity qualifies him for sonship; he can then run his father's business.

When we are born into the family of God as His children, God doesn't change just our environment; He also changes our bloodline. He delivers us from the power of darkness and translates us into the kingdom of His dear Son (Col. 1:13). He births us into His family.

To become adopted sons, however, who cry

"Abba, Father," who are heirs to the throne, we must come to maturity — increasing in wisdom and stature and receiving God's favor. Paul teaches clearly throughout the epistles that we are expected to become sons with knowledge. The Spirit of adoption, the Holy Spirit who lives inside us, enables us to come to mature sonship. He trains, nurtures and disciples us until we come to full stature.

Paul referred to this work of the Holy Spirit when he declared, "For all who are being led by the Spirit of God, these are sons of God" (Rom. 8:14, NAS). The discipline of being led by the Holy Spirit, receiving divine revelation from Him for all of life's situations, is the prerequisite for being called a son of God.

As we yield to the Spirit of adoption, we are trained as sons. As we continue to obey Him, He makes us heirs of God and joint heirs with Jesus Christ. One day He will let us rule with Him — when we are mature enough to reflect our Father's spirit, heart, vision and purpose.[1]

The Pattern Son Transfigured

Howbeit we speak wisdom among them that are perfect: yet not the wisdom of this world, nor of the princes of this world, that come to nought: But we speak the wisdom of God in a mystery, even the hidden wisdom, which God ordained before the world unto our glory (1 Cor. 2:6-7).

Paul refers to mature sons as those who "are perfect" and can hear the wisdom of God. He indicates that there is a mystery involved in the wisdom that

God reveals to His sons. That which has not been known becomes known through revelation as the veil is removed from our minds. Paul continues:

> But as it is written, Eye hath not seen, nor ear heard, neither have entered into the heart of man, the things which God hath prepared for them that love him. But God hath revealed them unto us by his Spirit: for the Spirit searcheth all things, yea, the deep things of God (1 Cor. 26:9-10).

God intends for us to know His divine purposes and all He has prepared for us from before the foundation of the world. But the only source of that information is revelation from the Spirit of God as He speaks to mature sons of God.

Recently the Holy Spirit spoke to me about the transfiguration of Jesus. I understood that God intends for believers to follow the pattern Son through the seven steps of redemption He walked while on earth. We are first to receive Christ's divine life by being born again, next to be water baptized and then to experience the baptism of the Holy Spirit.

The fourth step of redemption is to be led into the wilderness as Jesus was to overcome the enemy of our souls, defeating him as Jesus did when He declared, "It is written" (Matt. 4:4). Our wildernesses may take many forms — having to leave our relatives, friends, doctrinal positions, ambitions or plans to follow Christ. We can all testify to a place of temptation where we have had to establish our determination to worship God alone.

But how many of us have thought of the next step

in Jesus' life, that which took Him to the Mount of Transfiguration? It was there that He experienced the supernatural unveiling of the glory of God and heard the voice from heaven that once again affirmed, "This is my beloved Son in whom I am well pleased" (Matt. 17:5). Surely a similar experience does not occur in the lives of believers.

We understand that we will be required to go to the cross and be crucified with Christ in order to enjoy resurrection power. Thus of the seven steps of redemption, all but the fifth one, being transfigured, seem easy to apply to the life of the believer.

As I was meditating on the Scriptures, the Holy Spirit showed me that what was revealed in the transfiguration of Jesus was Adam as he would have become if he had not fallen. He would have become a mature son of God who pleased the Father in all that he did.

The Scriptures refer to Christ as the last Adam (1 Cor. 15:45). As Christ grew in favor with God and man and did His Father's will, He became the mature Son whom the Father could affirm. It was then that He entered into the ministry God had ordained for Him, directed by the Holy Spirit. Everything He did on earth was by the power of the Holy Spirit working through His humanity.

As I continued meditating on the wonder of the transfiguration, the Holy Spirit directed me to the book of Romans. He asked me what the word *transformed* meant in Romans 12:2. As I studied the word, I understood that it could be translated as "transfigured." It comes from the word *metamorphosis* and means to be changed or metamorphosed.

I began to weep and tremble as I saw the truth

God was making clear. In this verse the apostle Paul instructs us: "I beseech you therefore, brethren, by the mercies of God, that ye present your bodies a living sacrifice, holy, acceptable unto God which is your reasonable service...be ye transformed by the renewing of your mind" (Rom. 12:1-2). What he is really saying is for us to be transfigured by the power of the Holy Spirit living within us.

How is God going to fill our temples with His glory? When we surrender our bodies to Him as living sacrifices, we will become transfigured so the glory of God will be seen in us and shine forth through us. His Word, the Living Word, working in us His good pleasure will transform us so that the presence of God will shine forth from us. Then we will go forth in power, as Jesus did, to work the works of God that He has ordained for us to do.

The Glory of God

Many believers have a vague concept of the glory of God. Though it is referred to in the Scriptures hundreds of times, we have not always been able to define it clearly. Several different meanings for the glory of God need to be considered. However, the most simple definition of the glory of God is that it is His divine, manifest presence that dwells within us and is changing us as we yield to the work of the Holy Spirit. Paul declared that we were being changed "from glory to glory" (2 Cor. 3:18).

I trembled when I realized that this earthen vessel of mine, this temple of the Holy Ghost, can walk with God in such a way that it is filled with His glory — His manifest presence. I was so thrilled when I realized that the last Adam didn't lose the glory of God like the first one did. Jesus received everything in His humanity that the first Adam would have received if he had not fallen. If man had not fallen, God would have poured His glory — the weight of His divine presence — into man as He walked with him and communed with him. We witness in the transfiguration of Jesus the glory of God's presence as He had intended to give it to Adam.

Now, follow Christ to the garden of Gethsemane and listen to His prayer:

> And the glory which thou gavest me I have given them; that they may be one, even as we are one: I in them, and thou in me, that they may be made perfect in one; and that the world may know that thou hast sent me, and hast loved them, as thou hast loved me (John 17:22-23).

Jesus declared that He was praying not only for His disciples, but also for all who would believe on Him (v. 20). He wanted us to have the glory of God to fill our lives just as He had.

One day the Christ who dwells in the temple of believers — the church — will hear the divine voice of commendation again as the Father speaks, "These are my beloved sons, in whom I am well pleased." He will have a glorious church without spot or wrinkle, through which the glory of God will be manifest to the world. To this end, Paul prayed, "Unto him be glory in the church by Christ Jesus throughout all ages" (Eph. 3:21). Jesus is the Author and Finisher of our faith. He will walk the same path of redemption in us that He walked while on earth.

We will not be filled with His glory by having someone lay hands on us or prophesy over us. We will be transfigured as the Word of God becomes our life. As we allow our minds to be renewed, transforming our carnal thinking and perspective, and as we become filled with the divine revelation of the life of Christ, we will be able to say with Paul:

> I live; yet not I, but Christ liveth in me: and the life which I now live in the flesh I live by the faith of the Son of God who loved me, and gave himself for me (Gal. 2:20).

Jesus taught us the way to revelation in the simple statement, "Blessed are the pure in heart: for they shall see God" (Matt. 5:8). As we allow the precious Holy Spirit to fulfill His mandate in our lives, rending the veil of flesh and giving to us the things of Jesus, we will be filled with His glory (the manifested presence of God).

In that way, through the lives of believers, "the earth shall be filled with the knowledge of the glory of the Lord, as the waters cover the sea" (Hab. 2:14). Then we will see the word of the Lord fulfilled in us, "Arise, shine; for thy light is come, and the glory of the Lord is risen upon thee" (Is. 60:1).

The world will see the glory of God in His body as the disciples beheld the glory of God on the Mount of Transfiguration. The greatest days of the history of all Christendom are just ahead for the church. As the revelation of the Living Word becomes manifest in each of our lives, we will become the glorious church God intended us to be. My earnest prayer for the church today is powerfully expressed in the apostle Paul's prayer for all "the faithful in Christ Jesus" (Eph. 1:1):

> That the God of our Lord Jesus Christ, the Father of glory, may give unto you the spirit of wisdom and revelation in the knowledge of him: The eyes of your understanding being enlightened; that ye may know what is the hope of his calling, and what the riches of the glory of his inheritance in the saints, And what is the exceeding greatness of his power to us-ward who believe, according to the working of his mighty power,
>
> Which he wrought in Christ, when he raised him from the dead, and set him at his own right hand in the heavenly places, Far above all principality, and power, and might, and dominion, and every name that is named, not only in this world, but also in that which is to come (Eph. 1:17-21).

As the church grows to maturity, this divine life of Christ, the revelation of who He is in all His glory, will be seen by the world through believers. Our unity with God will result in our unity with one another. As we allow the Holy Spirit to divide asunder our souls and our spirits, Christ's love will be manifested toward one another and for a lost world. Not only will our lives be transformed, but also we will rejoice to see a great harvest of souls in answer to Jesus' prayer to the Father, "that the world may believe that thou hast sent me" (John 17:21).

When Jesus brings many sons to glory — sons with knowledge, those who cry "Abba, Father," and who are living by divine revelation, the prophet's declaration concerning Him will be fulfilled: "He shall see of the travail of His soul, and be satisfied" (Is. 53:11).

Notes

Chapter 2
Relationship Through Revelation

1. C. Austin Miles, "In the Garden" (© Hall-Mack Co., 1912: Renewed 1940 by the Rodeheaver Co. [a division of Word, Inc.]). All rights reserved.

Chapter 3
The Basis of All True Revelation

1. *The Works of John Wesley* (London, England: Wesleyan Methodist Book Room, 1872. Reprinted, Grand Rapids, Mich.: Baker Book House, 1979). In Fuchsia Pickett, *How to Search the Scriptures*, (Blountville, Tenn.: Fuchsia Pickett, 1972). Available from Fuchsia Pickett Ministries.

Chapter 4
How to Hear the Voice of God

1. Everett L. Worthington, Jr., *When Someone Asks For Help* (Downers Grove, Ill.: Intervarsity Press, 1982).

Chapter 5
The Language of Scripture

1. Fuchsia Pickett, *For Such a Time as This* (Shippensburg, Pa.: Destiny Image Publishers, 1992), 2-6.
2. Fuchsia Pickett, *The Prophetic Romance* (Lake Mary, Fla.: Creation House, 1996), 23-27.

Chapter 10
Transfiguration: The End of Revelation

1. Fuchsia Pickett, *Presenting the Holy Spirit* (Shippensburg, Pa.: Destiny Image Publishers, 1993), 91-94.

About the Author

D r. Pickett studied at John Wesley College and Virginia Bible College. She has an earned doctorate in the field of theology as well as a doctorate of divinity. She is an ordained minister, and pastored for twenty-seven years.

On April 12, 1959, God miraculously healed Dr. Pickett of a life-threatening disease and baptized her in the Holy Spirit.

Dr. Pickett has ministered as a conference evangelist and teacher and served as academic dean and director of a Bible college in Texas. She and her husband, Leroy, founded Fountain Gate Ministries in 1971. This ministry included an interdenominational church, preschool, academy and college as well as a nationwide tape lending library, video extension program, daily radio program and weekly television ministry.

Since 1988 Dr. Pickett has traveled extensively and is in great demand as a conference speaker, gifted teacher and author. She and her husband are based at Shekinah Ministries in Blountville, Tennessee.

Author of seven books that contain much of the revelation God has given her during almost fifty years of ministry, Dr. Pickett has also written more than twenty-five study manuals that are very helpful for ministers and lay people alike. She feels a divine mandate on her life to help train leaders to bring the church into the great revival that is coming.

Other Books by Fuchsia Pickett

God's Dream
The Eternal Purpose of God

For Such a Time As This
A Prophetic View of the Church

The Prophetic Romance
Timely Revelation from the Book of Ruth

The Next Move of God
Divine Revelation of the Coming Revival

Presenting the Holy Spirit (2 Volumes)
"Who Is He?" and "Walking in the Spirit"

To order the books listed above or to receive a free
catalog of resource materials including tapes, videos
and study manuals, call or write:

Fuchsia T. Pickett Ministries
394 Glory Road
Blountville, TN 37617
Phone: 423-279-9186
e-mail: fpickett@tricon.net

Visit Fuchsia Pickett on the Web
http://www.fuchsiapickett.com

If you enjoyed *Receiving Divine Revelation,* we would like to recommend the following books:

Praying With Smith Wigglesworth
by Larry Keefauver
In this unique prayer guide, Smith Wigglesworth's words are edited into dynamic prayers, thoughtfully arranged in a manner that Wigglesworth himself might have used. This book also includes a look into Smith Wigglesworth's prayer life and shows you how to become a prayer warrior for your family.

All in God's Time
by Iverna Tompkins
The road to our purpose in life, whether in our ministries, our careers or even our relationships, has been mapped out in ways we often don't understand...but God does. If you have ever wondered when your road to royalty as an heir of God's kingdom will end, then this book will encourage you to await, with patience and joy, the day of your coronation.

Available at your local Christian bookstore or from:

Creation House
600 Rinehart Rd.
Lake Mary, FL 32746
Phone: 407-333-3132
Fax: 407-333-7100
Web site: http:www//creationhouse.com